D0923579

SADISM IN THE MOVIES

GEORGE DE COULTERAY

SADISM
IN THE
MOVIES

TRANSLATED BY STEVE HULT : 1965
MEDICAL PRESS · NEW YORK

©COPYRIGHT 1965 MEDICAL PRESS OF N. Y.

PRINTED IN THE U.S.A.

CONTENTS

FOREWORD

Sadism in the movies exists only by a kind of miracle. The lofty thought of de Sade—this humanist who wrote only for men "capable of understanding", brilliantly challenged the natural human goodness over which his era sniveled, and replaced it with a comprehension of nature carried to its logical extreme—could scarcely be served by an art that prided itself on being popular and that sought to popularize itself by the basest means. Robert Benayoun's indignation is readily understood: "Every opportunity is used to invoke de Sade, whose glorious name sees itself constantly linked with ideas that he particularly abhorred. Sadistic is used more and more for torturing (Nazi-style); sadistic is used increasingly for neurotic *(the gangster sadist); when in actuality, Sade, paying (despite his passion for freedom) with 27 years imprisonment under three regimes, even risking death under the Terror, was the most lucid, best-balanced and most glorious of* moralists. *Between Sade and unnecessary cruelty, between Sade and brute violence, between Donatien-Alphonse-Francois and pathological excesses, there is a gulf as vast as that between the scattered stars of the heavens."*

In 1963, when confusion must have been particularly confounded, two men, Roger Vaillant, the script writer, and Roger

9

*Vadim, the director, who would modestly prefer to call them-
selves liberals, wrote and produced* Vice and Virtue *in which
the virtuous heroine was named Justine and the depraved one
Juliette; and in which they "honorably" acknowledged the
allusion to the Marquis' work. The simple fact that they had
seen in the Nazi regime the modern consequence of sadistic
thinking, and in the concentration camp the actualization of
the fulfilled universe of his desires, suffices to condemn an
enterprise (rather a cynical, commercial distortion) that does
not even have the excuse of ignorance or stupidity—at least
not in Vaillant's case.*

Still worse is that Vice and Virtue *seems to sanctify the
divorce between sadism and the cinema. This confusion between logical ecstacy and maniacal bureaucracy, between the
passionate desire to explore the limits of nature and the
striving for foolhardy impact could easily cause us to forget
fifty years of dreams, to slam the doors against more sincere
attempts, and make us despair.*

*Happily, this doesn't happen. The cinema is a miraculously
rich means of expression, so often pellucid, by its very naivete.
Its dreams proliferate through one of those marvelous processes that small minds believe they condemn by labelling them
"unintentional"; their exhibition* unites *the varied passions of
director and viewer, perfectly meeting de Sade's standard "as
minds corrupt each other in proportion to the nation's maturity, because nature is more deeply studied and better analyzed, so also to combat prejudices more effectively it is
imperative to be more familiar with them. This law is the
same for every art: it is only in maturing that they perfect
themselves." ("Thoughts on Novels"). And, similarly: "The
deep study of the heart of man, a labyrinth of nature, can only
inspire the novelist whose work must make us see man, not
only as he is, as he seems, (that is the duty of historians), but*

as that which he can be, to which the elaborations of vice and the transformations of his passions can restore him" ("Juliette"). If the screen does not offer, save for a few (all the more notable) exceptions, systematic exploration; if the 120 Days is yet to be filmed, its assiduous development offers enough situations, characters and plots to permit a montage of sadistic images.

But among the others, one man stands out, Bunuel. We will discuss him at length. But it is enough to recall that he was the only producer to make precise action of cruelty, and his importance will be established, all the more because only he, since the Golden Age, has never lost sight of the other vital dimension of sadism—love.

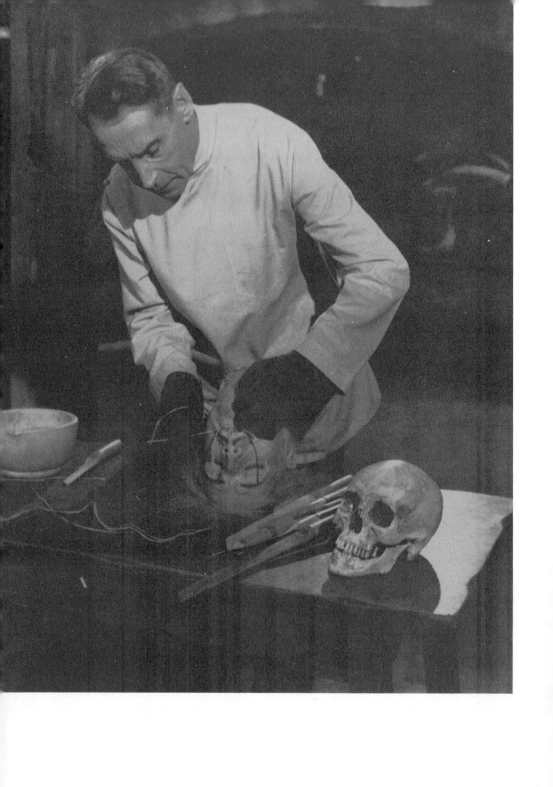

THE BRAWL

In movie history, a railroad employee was probably the first victim of violence. Felled by train robbers, the station-master of Edwin Porter's *Great Train Robbery* (1903) was the father of a long line of heroes who were put to sleep by blows from fists, blackjacks, butt-ends and diverse other contusive instruments.

For a long time, movie blows lacked great dramatic impact. To the viewer they seemed more like a slapping contest or a child's game than the ecstasy, where pain mixes with the pleasure, of seeing blows land on the opponent—pure pleasure and pain in the Kantian sense, since it transcends the gap from the screen. Movie fights were for a long time synonymous with gestures, as majestic as they were ineffective—right and left hooks which only a near-sighted and rheumatic cripple could not have evaded with the greatest ease.

The great epoch of the serial (the silent film whose praises are no longer sung) existed only during the embryonic period of pugilistic cinematography. *Zigomar, Nick Carter* or the *Vampires* (1908-1915) preferred intrigue to brutality. *Fantomas* and even *Judex* had too much intelligence and self-respect to condescend to slugging matches. They killed (exe-

15

cuting or avenging) with consistent elegance. Even in the
United States, where the rules and laws of violence were
secretly crystallizing, Pearl White—imprisoned, hanging, falling, on the verge of being crushed, burned or electrocuted—
always owed her safety to skill or luck, for, naturally, in these
sketches of triumphant womanhood the eternal good young
American boyfriend managed to come, late or inopportunely,
to Elaine or Pauline's rescue.

Came the age of Prohibition. The bootleggers, in order to
keep their hold on the city in which they distributed alcohol,
had, in addition to the traditional bomb through the window
(aimed rather at wares than at people), a choice of two
principal methods: to kill or to work over. From *Outside
the Law,* one of the first films in which Lon Chaney was
directed by Tod Browning, to *Scarface* by Hawks, and the
high point of this genre, Joseph Von Sternberg's *Chicago
Nights,* three decades saw the creation, glorification and
destruction of the myth of the gangster, who, outside the law,
is simultaneously both master and victim of the asphalt jungle,
a grandson of the Balzacian Ferragus. Concurrently, the
propmen put the finishing touches on a meticulously developed arsenal of breakaway objects, sugar glass and balsa wood
furniture, excellent for smashing, spectacularly but safely, on
the chest and loins of stunt men, to the maximum relish of
the spectator.

But the style and tactics for organizing this fun was very
erratic. Blows were never more than a means, an unsatis-
factory substitute, not an end in themselves. The breaking of
a jaw thus remained for *Jo-Jo,* and the best directors feel
this so strongly that they adroitly deflect attention by the
stylization, and the burlesque or humor of their fist-fights
and bar-room scenes. In the box-car of *Beggars of Life* the
brawl that breaks out among the hobos, is not really meant to

let anyone get hurt. The battle reduces itself to a series of gags which the great William Wellman commands with perfect serenity.

Rougher in nature, and representing more primitive types, who are therefore more disposed to settle their differences directly, Western heroes should have pitched into each other with more conviction. They are, supposedly, the direct descendants of prehistoric man, of *Man's Genesis* (1911 with Mae Marsh and Robert Harron), *Long Ago* (1931 with Bessie Eyton and William Oakman) and even, in a different key, *His Prehistoric Past* with Stan Laurel. What mismanagement! Neither the romantic "clear-eyed young man", William Hart, nor Harry Carey condescended to use his fists. For them adventure was an affair of honor and of nobility rather than of brute force. Therefore it is no surprise that the brawl between the heroes was the only weak point in the very beautiful *Wagon Train West* by Cruze.

In the movies as elsewhere, the apprenticeship of the punch is an affair of science and realism. From the magical reel of the nickleodeon to the cinematographic projection of *The Big Knife* (Robert Aldrich, 1955) as in *The Ring* (Alfred Hitchcock, 1927), Raoul Walsh's *Gentleman Jim,* where Errol Flynn played the part of a boxer of the heroic period, *The Set Up* by Robert Wise, and *Champion* (Mark Robeson) to cite only a few titles, the exchanges follow the rules of the noble art: the slugging match, the saving bell, and the bloody and swelling faces.

Among these films *The Set Up* should receive special notice, partly because of its background of gangsterism, which permitted violence to pass beyond the ropes, and partly because it had a sordid ending, and was much more effective than a boxing movie. Here it is less a question of the triumphant career of the steel-fisted champion—or clay-fisted champion,

as in *The Man With Clay Fists* (L'homme aux poings d'argile)
an insignificant film to the credit of Marcel Cerdan—but
of a has-been boxer (Robert Ryan) who is paid to take a
dive, but who, in an upsurge of dignity, fights honestly at the
end. The admirable, mobile camera of Robert Wise revolves
around the boxers. The blows thud on faces moist with sweat
and blood that spurt under the impact, and shine in the raw
lights of projectors. It is understood that faced with a similar
prospect of inevitable pain and enduring courage, less strong-
minded fighters than the hero find a frantic refuge in prayer
before combat.

If the cinema had come to perfect the rules of brutality
within the frame of boxing, it was by consulting boxing pro-
fessionals to authenticate its brawls. Thus, in Borzage's *The
Big City,* a movie about New York taxi-drivers, Spencer Tracy
found himself clouted by ex-heavyweight champion Jack
Dempsey. The final set-to achieved a violence and a verisimilitude which made 1937 an important date in the history
of film fights.

While technique was being perfected, the pretexts were
being strengthened and organized with the birth and molding
into form of the "black" film. Of course, other styles profited
from these improvements and no one can either ignore or
forget the Homeric free-for-alls in *Shane* (George Stevens,
1953) or *These Thousand Hills* (Richard Fleischer, 1958);
but their violence still keeps the justification for force the
wholesome, rural way of life, as the Irish brutality which
John Ford depicted knowledgeably and joyously as the vicissitudes of life in *The Quiet Man,* (1953). Of a completely
different flavor is the violence which appears with the third,
the best type, *The Maltese Falcon* (John Huston, 1941) and
with the first version of *High Sierra* (Raoul Walsh, 1941).
Instead of the supermen of the 20's, and the ingenious police-

men of the 30's, a race of modern heroes is born with complex goals and motives, filled with a vague, melancholy thirst like that of Fonda in *You Only Live Once* (Fritz Lang, 1937). For these heroes, brutality is not simply an accident, but that for which they train or suffer, as their natural contact with the world; it is their way of life.

If it is necessary to stress *The Big Sleep* and, especially, *Dead Reckoning* completed within a year of each other (1946, 1947), it is because they elevate to the ranks of the rough-stuff heroes an actor who had already been famous for ten years: Humphrey Bogart. Dick Powell had seemed to be on the wrong track in the role of the drugged and bludgeoned hero in Edward Dmytryk's feeble *Murder My Sweet*. But Humphrey Bogart, whose lengthy criminal education directed by Lewis Seiler (*Men Without Law,* 1937, *Crime School*) and, above all, Lloyd Bacon (*The Revolt* 1935, *Marked Woman* 1937) and William Wyler (*Dead End*), had already established this new law, found in *The Maltese Falcon* where, beaten by Sidney Greenstreet's thugs, he faced the brutality that was going to become his daily bread, that the hero would often get the worst of it, deserted by the miracles of his invincible physical vitality. Therefore, in *The Big Sleep* Marlowe-Bogart, a strictly dream version of the Dashiell Hammett characters, is by the novelist Chandler and by Faulkner, Furthman and Brackett the scriptwriters, and finally by Hawkes the stage director, placed on the maniacal path that promises the greatest opportunities to get beaten up. From the short and savage battles which punctuate, by their light of pain, a universe pledged to darkness, he emerges swollen and bloody, to kiss Lauren Bacall's pouting lips, that offer the eroticism that is reserved only for him.

Dead Reckoning (John Cromwell), which some hold to be one of the peaks of style, goes even further. It was necessary

to see the hero barely half-conscious drag himself along, try
to stand up again while clinging to a desk, and being beaten
yet again, to establish that henceforth true courage, and thus
dignity, do not always consist in being the strongest, but in
knowing how to endure violence. This was recognized elsewhere, by the descendants of Dashiell Hammett's *The Glass
Key* which has two adaptations, the first in the 30's with
George Raft, and the second, directed by Stuart Heisler, in
1942, with Alan Ladd. Raymond Borde and Etienne Chau-
meton thus describe the most famous scene in the film: "As
the anonymous review in the exhibitor's guide says: 'as re-
gards fists fights, Alan Ladd gets more than he gives.' In
fact he is the subject of the most sensational shellacking in
the movies. Periodically, with machine-like regularity, his
warders worked him over. He no longer has a human face;
he is a paper doll, crushed, ripped, and dirty. He attempts to
move. They beat him and throw him in a filled bathtub. One
torturer announces: 'Well, he's floating.' The thugs dump
him on a shabby bed and pick up their card-hands again."
(*Panorama of the American Black Film*).

In the history of the working-over, in the movies as elsewhere, it is natural that the police play a large role; that
they utilize the "nail-bag"—even our own police who tortured Bernard Blier in Clouzot's (*Goldsmith's Dock*) *Quai
Des Orfevres*—or the American third degree, or better still
the specialties cultivated by the police of other countries.
Certainly the movies usually placed greater emphasis on
scientific methods of detection than on the strongarm method
of obtaining confessions, as in *Mystery Street* (John Sturges,
1950) and the *Enforcer* (Bretaigne Windust, 1950), but
there are enough debatable exceptions, on the whole, as to
their secret ethics. *On Dangerous Ground* (Nicholas Ray
1951) as well as *Detective Story* (William Wyler, 1951) at

first glance seem to be condemning usual police methods when it is necessary to obtain "the gentlest confession". But this is only on the surface, and William like Nicholas, was concerned with evading, if not justifying. On the one hand they dwell on the absolute villainy of the guilty, who deserve any punishment, and on the other, the neurotic state of the police, overburdened with their responsibilities, or who see their buddies succumb to gangsters' blows. Certainly there are black sheep, but these are isolated cases, exculpable, and subjects for psychological study, not sociological morality.

Prison warders have been spared less than the cops, from Mervyn Le Roy's *I Am a Fugitive* (1932) to Jules Dassin's *Brute Force* (1947), and also William Keighley *Each Dawn I Die* (1939), Cahn's *Le Bagnard,* and others, *Blackmail* (H. C. Porter) and *Prison Without Bars* excluded (these are about convicts who are ladies—and French). Recall Paul Muni beaten, and Hume Cronyn, Hitler-style bludgeoner, heading towards his victim tied in a chair, to the accompaniment of Wagnerian music. This explains and even justifies the flaming savagery that marks the typical prison rebellion. The classic model *Big House* (George Hill, 1930), a little overrated for the type, is however, careful not to go too far, since the good chief-warden will be protected from the savage wrath of the convicts by none other than the upright prisoner who thus rehabilitates himself.

But, in general, the craft of dealing out blows remains the privilege of outlaws, savages, and half-savages. Society, even in its purely repressive activities, uses it only rarely and regretfully, or by accident. Society has hardly anything to do with violence. Is it not done in the name of virtue and justice?

Even when not mortal, physical wounds furnish a fine dramatic springboard. The hero of *Ride the Pink Horse* (1947), interpreted by Robert Montgomery, manages to drag himself along for a good part of the film, his back gaping open from a knife wound; the wounding, by the way, is a masterpiece of cold-blooded cruelty. Similarly, the wounded revolutionary in *Odd Man Out* (Carol Reed, 1947) is in his death throes during virtually the entire film, morbid proof of the steadfastness of the English soul. Jean Gabin in *Pepe Lo Moko* (Jules Dassin, 1938) barely had the strength to go down a flight of stairs (a long flight to be sure), of the Algerian Casbah. Stronger still, in *He Walked by Night* (Alfred Werker, 1948), Richard Basehart, wounded, finds the strength to remove the bullet from his own arm.

Ordinarily the blind are a paradoxical object of emotion in the movies. From Bette Davis' *Victory Over Night* (Edmund Golding, 1939) to Sacha Guitry's *Give Me Your Eyes* (1942) the blind are only the pretext for saccharine pity. But blindness itself, when it results from violence of events and men, evokes another sort of emotion. The mechanic in *The Wheel* (*La Roue*, Abel Gance, 1922), the various misadventures of Michael Strogoff (from Essenay's 1908 version to that of Carmine Gallone in 1956 and the six or seven intermediate reworkings) all contrive to blind him with equal relish or joy (if we may use that word). On the steps of Odessa the combination of a broken eyeglass and the blood-tinged pulp which flows from the eye-socket gives Eisenstein the premise for one of the most truly shocking shots in the whole history of the movies (*Potemkin*, 1925). *Andalusian Dog*, (*Un Chien Andalou*, Luis Bunuel and Salvador Dali, 1928) begins with the famous sequence of the razor slicing out an eye. Bela Lugosi in Edgar G. Ulmer's *The Black Cat* (1934) gouges out the eye of a cat. In *The Vikings* (Richard *Fleischer,* 1958), Tony Curtis hurls a trained falcon to peck out Kirk Douglas' eyes. A sequence by Maurice Labo (*Immediate Action,* 1957) shows, with calculated tranquilness, the point of a chisel nearing an eye that is staring out of the victim's head.

The science of amputation in the film is even richer. Usually, and for reasons of censorship, it is the limbs that get cut off, preferably the hands.

Howard Hawks has proved that confining oneself to the finger can still achieve effective scenes in this genre. In *The Big Sky* (1941) the focus on the amputation of Kirk Douglas' finger is the best sequence of the film. The hero carefully gets drunk, and finds himself at the end of the scene, stupidly truculent as could be wished, with one finger less. Hawks very skilfully knew how to paint the strange attractive fear of physical pain and, thanks to a careful slowness, created a new, and assuredly very stimulating style of suspense.

Cut-off hands dot the history of the movies. In Tod Browning's *The Unknown,* Lon Chaney cuts off his arms to please the woman he loves. In *The Vikings,* not only is Tony Curtis deprived of one of his wrists, but he watches the wound being cauterized with a red-hot iron. In *The Hand of the Devil* (Maurice Tourner, 1941) Pierre Fresnay, howling, sees himself robbed of his right hand by a force from another world. However, it is not always necessary to cut, since it is possible to crush with a blow from a brick (*The Set Up*) or to shred with a bullet, *The Man From Laramie* (Anthony Mann, 1925). *Attack* (Robert Aldrich, 1957) shows a tanktread roll over Jack Palance's arm as he agonizedly writhes in the mud, his arm torn and dripping blood. Finally, recall the plea which broke forth at each new adaptation of *Cheri-Bibi* from Mathot to Pagliero, dismal enough in itself: "No, not the hands! Not the hands!"

Cruelty of this sort is felt the more keenly since the hands are a privileged erotic object. It was because Joan Crawford had a morbid repugnance about hands that Lon Chney mutilated himself in *The Unknown*. In the fantasies, hands can be animated with an independent life in order to perpetrate strange atrocities, or to be haloed with a weird sensual aura. The many versions of *Hands of Orlac* (*Mains d'Orlac*), Robert Wiene's as well as that of Karl Freund (entitled *Mad Love*) and Edmund T. Greville, are full of these seductions. In another fashion, Robert Florey's film *The Beast With Five Fingers* (1940) contains a highly extraordinary and perverse love duo, Peter Lorre and a severed hand animated by supernatural life. Thus, no one among the passersby is very startled when in the *Andalusian Dog* a young woman, dreamy and indifferent to the crowd around her, plays with a severed hand. It is far from the horror aroused **in Fay Wray** in *Doctor X,* when, naked and tied to the operating table, she sees a one-armed mad scientist adjust a scientifically animated hand to his stump.

Amputating and blinding have a close relation with the art of disfiguring. All instrumentalities are satisfactory: physical, as the broken bottles in *Vera Cruz,* and *From Here To Eternity*: chemical, as the acid, which Erik gets smack in the face in the many versions of *Phantom of the Opera,* but which misses Charlton Heston in *Touch of Evil*: or even heat, like the boiling coffee which disfigures Gloria Graham in *The Big Heat.*

Surgical wounds are more deliberate and of purer intent. They are, at first, the subject of educational films and restricted documentaries. Surgical films (now in color), are principally a tool for study, reserved for practitioners, their brutalness as well as their technical details rendering them inappropriate for the elderly or for movie-going future patients. Considered as proper for popular consumption are only such works as *Leriche, Surgeon of Pain* (Paul Pivot), or *Diagnostic CIV* and *You Will Give Birth Without Pain* (Fabiani) the subject of which was described exactly by Francois Michel: "Thus, here is a film with completely new aims, since it proposes to modify 'thought, a cerebral secretion', pain being considered an inferior level of consciousness" ("Positif," No. 21, p. 40). Certain producers, as professional showmen and foxy thinkers, nevertheless know what fascination still-warm flesh, exposed and scientifically worked over, has for "the masses". (From the novels by Van der Meersch, Frank Slaughter and other Soubirans.) Duvrier in *Under the Bridges of Paris* therefore inserts in his montage shots showing an operation where an open heart is brilliantly removed. The same Duvrier knew how to play on the horror inspired by Pierre Blanchard who, as an abortionist, sterilizes his nickle-plated instruments by thrusting them into blazing alcohol (*Carnet de Bal* 1937). Subtler and more honest, Capra also shrewdly has the medical bag gleam with surgical instruments, when opened by a sneering Peter Lorre; but this scene, which achieved the utmost laughter and shock, as completely as could be desired, was far from reaching the effectiveness attained by Delmer Davis in *Dark Passage* (1945) where the subjective camera admirably depicts the anguish of Humphrey Bogart undergoing plastic surgery by a quack doctor. Medicine has other weapons, which are used by the shocking Dr. Crespi (*The Crime of Dr. Crespi,* John Auer, 1935), as well as by Gerard Philippe, an alcoholic doctor in Yves Allegret's *The Proud and the Damned,* who performs a painful and delicate spinal injection without sparing the viewer the slightest detail. And still to be recounted are the innumerable childbirth scenes which permit the harmonious union of tenderness for the newly-born, with the agony of the parturient women, from *Gone with the Wind* (Victor Fleming, 1939), to *Brink of Life* (Ingmar Bergman, 1957); these include *All My Babies* (George Stoney, 1959) and *Le Beau Serge* (Claude Chabrol, 1957).

When animals are involved, scruples become legitimately less profound. The greatest experimenters are those whose emotions are the most effectively anesthesized, the Soviets. In 1925, Pudovkin inaugurated his career as a producer with a documentary on *The Mechanism of the Brain,* dedicated to the glory of Pavlovian methods and principles, where dogs played a large if not a magnificent role. The famous fistula operation was filmed again by Rochal (*Pavlov, the Academicien,* 1949). There could even be seen in France (fugitively, since the newsreels in which it appeared were quickly censored) the severed heads of dogs placed on a platter, with the blood vessels connected to nutritive tubes, barking and blinking their eyes—all this going one better than the ancient, merry crew of saints who carried about their own severed heads. *Mechanical Butchery* depicted by Georges Sadoul was less scientific ("History of World Cinema", p. 22) and more humane, and without too much attention to the hypocritical tears so dear to the SPCA, there are various films by Georges Franju. *Animals' Blood* (1948) about the slaughterhouses of La Villette, was thus described by Freddy Buache: "We enter into the subject by shots which are reminiscent of Carne, but slowly behind these images of sad suburbs where the most absurd objects of bric-a-brac sparkle, an anguish is insinuated, which bursts forth in the terrible face of a white horse being felled. Then we advance into full nightmare; but at each step by a factual detail, by the consideration of a cold, utilitarian technique (inventory of tools) by a gentle comment (the boy who cleaves a side of beef to the twelve strokes of noon), by an historic reference (the portrait of Auguste Macquart) Franju reminds us that this is not a nightmare and that in the shadow of the steeple of this false church, a false cult holds its ceremonies with good conscience and innocence. The systematic butchery of livestock because man must live, and so that he can enjoy fillet steak and beef brains in vinegar. ("Premiere Plan," no. 1. p. 8) *The Salmon of the Atlantic* (1955) where the scenic charm of the shoreline contrasts with the bloody salmon-fishing, and *My Dog* (about fur), testify to similar preoccupations as remote from superfluous cruelty as from too readily-aroused pity.

The career of vivisection in the movies is not too rich but has at least one success: Erle C. Henton's *Island of Lost Souls*. According to Ado Kyrou: "Doctor Moreau, in the guise of Charles Laughton, transforms animals into men and women by horrible vivisections. His masterpiece is Lota, superb panther-woman (Kathleen Burke). This animal-woman (in love with Richard Arlen who battles with the monster Gola, the ape man) rebelling against her master who has forgotten her original feline nature, is a perfect expression of feminine eroticism in its pure state" ("Eroticisme et Cinema," p. 238).

In fact, as a general rule, it is in the para-scientific domain of the shocker that surgery, most frequently mad, manages to sharpen its lancet most horribly. The first version of *Frankenstein,* the tale of a monster made from various fragments of corpses, was more concerned with the creature's atrocities than with the quest for these pieces and assembling them into a new being. This search is the original element in the films by the Englishman Terence Fisher: *The Curse of Frankenstein* (1957) and the *Revenge of Frankenstein* (1958), especially the first. With the aid of technicolor, no one could forget the grease-cased, blood-moist eyes that Christopher Lee dropped in the jar, nor the arms which he unpacked with care from between red-stained tissue. The recent upsurge of H (for horror) movies appears to have found a nourishing resource in surgery and dissection. In the United States, Curt Siodmak had already imagined the adventures and evil deeds of his *Donovan's Brain,* a brain severed from the body of its owner. But the organ wisely stayed in a crystal vessel filled with nourishing fluids and acted only through telepathy. By contrast, Arthur Crabtree's *Fiend without a Face,* can creep, by means of the spinal cord he still possesses, and since he can move about is able to launch himself at his victim's head. The *Trollenberg Terror* recounts the vicissitudes of a head completely severed from its body.

The sons of Dr. Moreau, if not of Frankenstein (although *Frankenstein 70* and his scarcely credible operations permit the forecasting of little Frankensteins) nowadays have more modest ambitions, and pleasanter if less metaphysical intentions. They are becoming plastic surgeons. Thanks to his art, the hero of *Circus of Horror* (Sidney Hayers, 1960) can surround himself with a willing harem, made to order. He is happier than Edith Scob's father, Pierre Brasseur who sought to remake the face of his disfigured child and therefore used as grafts the features of many pretty girls, but never successfully. Georges Franju's *Eyes without a Face,* which traced the history of these set-backs, contained two scenes whose chilling horror was quite astonishing. In an earlier film, (*The Head Against the Walls;* La Tete Contra Les Murs) he had not hesitated to show a madman scarred by a blow from a compass saw; this time he follows the scalpel that traces around the face, makes the forceps, which loosen the skin, glint, and afterwards allows the living flesh to be admired. Finally, elsewhere, bordering on the unbearable, he runs a series of still shots of the different stages of decompostion that beset Edith Scob's admirable face.

One could not conclude a discussion of operations without saying a word about several others, more harmless in appearance. They involve dentistry. Usually, in the movies, dentists are heroes of comedies rather than instigators of bloody dramas. Their prototype is well-personified by Bob Hope in *Paleface* (Norman Z. MacLeod, based on a scenario by Frank Tashin) who in a Western outfit lugs around both his clinical inexperience and his laughing gas. From the early masters, Georges Sadoul cites the fabulous *Doctor Colton Anesthesizing with Gas and Pulling a Tooth* (op. cit. p. 17 and *This Rotten Tooth* (op. cit. p. 41). Preston Sturges' first film, *The Great McGinty* sent a toothpuller to the senate. Nothing in all this transcended the level of everyday fear; therefore to signal an exception, it was necessary to call on all Stroheim's prestige to provide pleasure for those that certified there was an evil intent in the buccal speleology and the bloody stumps.

DEATH

No one committed suicide by throwing himself under a train in La Ciotat Station. The barge did not sink while weathering the jetty. The workers walking out of the factory did not launch a revolutionary attack, and society did not shoot them down. Baby did not strangle while eating his soup.

This is just an oversight. In the history of the movies violent death has a privileged place, perhaps the highest.

COLD STEEL

Credit where credit is due. Medieval cold steel is a perfect point of departure to usher in, logically and historically, the pomp of cinematic massacre. The *Assassination of the Duke of Guise* (L'Assassinat du Duc de Guise) was recreated in 1908 by Le Bargy and Calmettes, based on a script by Academician Lavendan. As Georges Sadoul notes with his customary penetration: "Bloody violence was a sure spice."

From the time of this pioneer film, if not the first of its type at least the most polished, duels and murder by cold steel were destined to become one of the most fertile sources of movies. The long line of cape and sword spectacles has not yet ended, no more than have the reconstructions of more ancient scenes.

Thus, in the episode of the fall of Babylon in Griffith's

33

Intolerance (1916) one sees a warrior cleanly sliced in two, lengthwise, by a single stroke of the sword, in the best tradition of the troubadour epics. In 1958, a man is killed, a subtle refinement, by the mere stub of a sword (*The Vikings*); From that early date up to now the filmography of cold steel is quite rich.

Douglas Fairbanks' movies always focus on a blade: the sword of the *Three Musketeers,* the dagger with which he threatens the loins of the already greatly tortured Anne May Wong in *Black Pirate,* the sabre of *The Thief of Bagdad,* and finally the semi-anachronistic sword—we are now close to the historical and esthetic frontiers of the Western—of the *Mark of Zorro* and *Don Q, Son of Zorro,* more knightly than the revolver that waits in the wings. Doug also personified *Robin Hood* the subject of countless remakes, from which pile the Michael Curtis' 1937 film, with Errol Flynn, should be extracted. In the final duel, involving flights of stairs, over-turned furniture and chandeliers, we are not spared a single detail: then, for the traitor's death, the sword of the lover of justice plunges several inches into the chest, and the face of the ghastly vicim convulses with a very believable grimace of agony.

In a genre that is difficult, because it is poorly adapted to innovation, some directors knew how to prove their undeni-able originality. Jacques Demeure (in the 14-15 number of "Positif") in an article of extreme, let's say, historical, im-portance (since it foreshadowed by a good few years, the earnest passion of certain critics for the Italian cinema) described with understandable emotion, the best moment in *Under the Bridge of Sighs*; "the chief attraction of the film is without doubt the duel of the two girls, in long white gowns in the garden of the institution (the film unfolds, in the Eighteenth Century, in a girl's boarding school). In the dead of night an extraordinary striptease takes place at sword-point. The impact of the scene is naturally intensified by the wind, rain, lightning, and the varied storm elements manifested throughout the film (p. 125-126)."

Orson Welles had harmoniously joined the joys of the mechanical with the seductions of cold steel. In *The Stranger* (1946) he had, with a diverting sense of the arbitrary, included a church clock with mechanical figures, for the sole purpose of having a Nazi run-through by an archangel bearing a sword of justice. Prompted by the same concern for novelty and innovation, Nathan Juran has Sinbad cross swords with a skeleton, in the best sequence of *The Seventh Voyage of Sinbad*.

Because the last world war put a high value on commando fighting, the dagger was able to achieve here, midway in the twentieth century, an unforeseen "freedom of the city". The bayonet had already been in existence for several centuries, but no film has yet related in much detail the glory of this trench cleaner, the cutlass specialist whose image Franju hails in a roundabout way in his *Hotel Des Invalides* (1951). The 40's came, and we see in the submarine that lands a handful of men to attack an island, soldiers sharpening their daggers with jealous care (Ray Enright's *Gung Ho!*). They stop polishing only when satisfied that they can split a hair with a single stroke. The parachutists of *Battalions from the Sky* (Bataillons du ciel, Alexandre Esway) use these daggers with unsurpassed virtuosity, not only to kill German soldiers, but to pin a flag against the wall of the pub in the British town where they are garrisoned. But it is the great superiority of *Destination Burma* (Raoul Walsh, 1945) that deserves the medal. To kill a Jap who is bending over a stream to fill a bucket with water, Errol Flynn begins by throwing a dagger that lands between his shoulderblades. The poor victim, on the very brink of death, turns around just in time to have a second dagger, thrown from an equally sure hand, pierce his chest.

Still more recently, the exploits of teenage criminals have brought a new variant to the glory of cold steel: the switch-blade whose blade automatically springs out when the appropriate button is pushed. It doesn't take a great psychoanalyst to guess what frustrations and desire are hidden behind this symbol. The crime discussed by the *Twelve Angry Men* (Sydney Lumet, 1956) was committed with just such a weapon. It is kept in full view, stuck upright in the table, through most of the film. And again, James Dean, in *Rebel Without a Cause* (Nicholas Ray, 1955), in fighting with a switchblade uses, as the German student does his sabre, the edge rather than the point. Lastly, it is with this same knife, for example, that the murder is committed in (*23 Paces to Bleecker Street,* Hathaway) and with which Vic Morrow will threaten his teacher, Glenn Ford, in *Blackboard Jungle* (Richard Brooks, 1955).

Although as we have seen, they can occasionally be used as throwing weapons, knives, sabres and swords should leave this work to more appropriate instruments: javelins and arrows. But note that there is one variant of the javelin, the lance, which despite its name should never leave the user's hand, and which has a place in spectacles about antiquity, from *Passion* (Zecca and Nonguet, 1903) to the modern *Spartacus* (Stanley Kubrick, 1960), including the many versions of the *Ten Commandments* and other films by the always biblical Cecil B. DeMille (1924, 1956). Note also so exotic an evocation as the splendid and unappreciated *Toura, Goddess of the Jungle* (Georges Archaimbaud, 1937), at which we must pause for a moment. The beautiful priestess, Dorothy Lamour, of a cult as pagan as it is evil, is caged in a reed sarcophagus that the grand priest of this cult, possessed by a high frenzy, pierces through with the spears of her native guards.

Indians, also savages as everyone knows, use this weapon, when the opportunity arises, as adroitly as a Bengal Lancer. They use it from horseback, in trying to impale Richard Widmark in *The Last Wagon* (Delmer Davis, 1955). Conversely, Patricia Owen stabs, with his own spear, a redskin who is about to kill Robert Ryan in *The Treasure of the Hanged* (Robert Sturges, 1957). The Romans also knew how to use the pilum quite skilfully, demonstrating that fact in *Julius Caesar* (Guazzoni) and in the various versions of *Quo Vadis* (by Zecca or by Mervyn Le Roy) which lead the innumerable battalions of period films, in peplum or biblical garb, that use the boar-spear as if it were a lance.

The arrow: a weapon as black as it is yellow, but especially red, since splashed with war paint it is one of the decorations of the Western. Its force is too little appreciated—the simple fact should be considered that it was used with very happy effect even after the weapon traders had distributed brand-new Winchesters and Martins to the tribes at death's door. An episode of *Winchester 75* (Anthony Mann) is the best evidence for those who see in it little more than an improvement on an earlier prehistoric weapon.

In fact, a good arrow shot was capable of puncturing the brainpan, and even a steel plaque, as surely as a piece of nickle-plated lead. Its fire-power spurred Colonel Colt to invent, and then perfect, the weapon named after him, in order to restore the strategic equilibrium which had been badly compromised by the revolver's lack of precision. Besides, the arrow's barbs made its extraction very difficult. Short of being an accredited surgeon, one had to cut it out with a razor rather than pull it loose. There are scenes of this almost impossible extraction, difficult even for specialists, in *Wagon Train West* (Cruze), and in *She Wore A Yellow Ribbon* (John Ford, 1949), where the operation is set off by a beautiful stormy sky, and in *Stagecoach* (John Ford, 1939).

Very often, the Indian attack is signaled by the sudden collapse of the sentinel or the rearguard, a long, feathered and painted shaft stuck in his chest or, better still, in his throat, to prevent his sounding the alarm, as in *Drums Along the Mohawk* (John Ford). One original twist in *Run of the Arrow* (Samuel Fuller) is to set fire to these arrows before loosing them on the Yankee cavalry troop. Thus, a soldier peacefully seated in the rear of the last wagon in the train, can experience a brand burying itself between his shoulder blades; and later the devastated army fort is strewn with bodies still bearing these smoldering firebrands. The arrow, even without flame, as St. Sebastian well knows, provides a pretext for very interesting esthetic effects. In *Treasure of the Hanged* a white killer gets an arrow square in his chest, but still advances, firing at his enemies, and collapses when pierced by a second projectile, thus becoming the modern brother of the highly picturesque, riddled captives who, in homage to Sodom, drape themselves over the ramparts of Kazan in Eisenstein's *Ivan the Terrible* (Part I).

And yet the redskins continue to find uses for the arrow, as original as they are ingenious. The great ballistics expert, John Sturges, shows them at Fort Bravo, as skilful in the art killing with these parabolic shots, without exposing themselves, as the most bemedaled artillery crack shot. For them, the arrow is often more than a weapon; it is a language. Painted in tribal colors, decorated with meaningful baubles, and thrust in the earth at the correct spot to inform the knowledgable scout, that the Comanches, the Sioux or the

Apaches are on the warpath. This weapon is also the pretext for an ingeniously conceived game, the rules of which are set forth in Fuller's *Run of the Arrow*. You choose a terrain, preferably bare and stony; you disarm your opponent; you take off his shoes, and you place him on the starting line. You shoot an arrow, and let the enemy advance to the point where it falls. When he reaches it, you hurl yourself in pursuit, and run him an unequal race, since he is barefooted and weaponless, while you are shod and have your bow. He runs and runs; that is all he can do.

The medieval archers brought much of science and many almost poetic inventions to their barbaric craft. The tactic in Laurence Olivier's *Henry V*, perhaps new to the battle of Agincourt, has been far surpassed by the least of the Apaches. To all intents and purposes, it remains only for the man of the Middle Ages to apply himself. Thus, in Jacques Tourneur's *The Flame and the Arrow*, Burt Lancaster can show an unparalleled skill. In *Robin Hood*, Errol Flynn surpasses all possible rivals by splitting in two the arrow which his opponent had already shot into the dead center of the target.

Let us note, in concluding with the sons, cousins, and disciples of *William Tell* (Lucien Nonguet, 1903) that now in mid-twentieth century, the bow is still the favorite of some dilettantes. In a remake of Count Zaroff's hunts, that is, *Game of Death* (Robert Wise), the hero is a devotee of the feathered shaft.

FIREARMS

The beginning for firearms was like that of the bow. Both were born in the same year, in the same country, at the time of *The Great Train Robbery*. It is certainly possible to point out, here as elsewhere, that the role of the nickleodeon was very important and that, thanks to it, authentic pictures of Annie Oakley were preserved, long before *Annie Get Your Gun* was dedicated to the biography of her legend. Curious minds will even recall that one of the earliest cameras we owe to Marey's fertile genius, had the shape of a double-barreled shotgun. It remains to note that gunfire was first exchanged in the wholesome atmosphere of a smoky train, and in saloons equipped with painted ladies, in short, the Western.

Weapons of the Western

If Jean-Louis Rieupeyrout has the great merit of having underlined the importance of the historical components of the Western, he was perhaps wrong not to have noted the great concern for authenticity in the weapons. When one is familiar with the success which greeted all the publications, (the voluminous *Gun Digest* is the prototype) that treat of portable firearms and their history; when one knows the glory attached to museums whose sole purpose is to trace the history of the American gun from 1850 to 1900; when finally one is assured that Anthony Mann had recourse to such a museum in arming the heroes of *The Man From Laramie,* then one will hardly be surprised that the fascination surrounding the entire saga of the West shows such purity and faithfulness to the technical aspects.

Everything begins with James Fenimore Cooper's long deer rifle. This would be the concern of *Northwest Passage* (King Vidor, 1940), *Unconquered* (Cecil B. DeMille, 1949), *Drums Along the Mohawk* (previously cited) *Big Sky* (Howard Hawks) or *Across the Wide Missouri* (William Wellman, 1949). None of these pre-Westerns, as Westerns set prior to 1840-1850 are known, fails to conform to the panoply popularized by Davy Crockett: inordinately long gun, hammer equipped with flint, powder-horn and bullet pouch. If the Napoleonic cartridge had not yet crossed the sea, virtuosity was none the less master of the land. In an even more recent period piece, the eve of the first World War, one of these primitive weapons, whose heritage is reverently preserved, is used by Gary Cooper in *Sergeant York* (Hawks, 1941)—having rejoined the army and become a ruthless killer—to behead turkeys at 100 paces, first wetting the barrel-end so that the reflection on the metal won't interfere with the accuracy of the aim.

A double revolution occurred. The first followed the production of the assembly-line revolver (Colt 45); the second the invention of the famous Winchester repeater rifle and of its rival, the Martin rifle.

The ordinary "frontier" or the long-barrelled "peacemaker" Colt from the eminence of its 45 calibre, is the essential element in Western mythology. Its holster hanging at mid-thigh strapped down to assure steadiness for the "draw", has historical origins as strongly rooted in tradition as the horn handle, and its specialist techniques.

A rather inaccurate weapon, at least at first, traditionally it was drawn only in hand-to-hand tussles, and the most skilful was, less the most accurate shot, than the first and the fastest shot. What was the origin of these strange sexual routines in which the partners looked each other over, legs planted apart to assure their balance, the right hand, fingers extended or leisurely contracted, depending on the rules, poised just above the butt, waiting for the least sign of cracking on the part of the opponent? Of the innumerable titles, some at least must be cited: *The Gunfighter* (Henry King, 1949), in which the hero, Gregory Peck, finds himself forced by his renown as "the fastest gun in the West" into duels which disgust him more and more; *The Outlaw* (Howard Hughes), in which the heroes take a curious pleasure in cutting off each other's ears by shots from their Colts; *Shotgun* (Lesley Selander); *The Fastest Gun Alive* (Russell Rouse) (this title, as Roger Tailleur qute accurately pointed out, is a pleonasm) ("Positif" No. 22, p. 22), *Man Without a Star* (King Vidor), in which a young future killer, full of pride in his brand-new talent, provokes a fight with just anyone, to prove he is the fastest, and ruthlessly kills. *Johnny Guitar,* where Johnny tosses his pistol from hand to hand like a too-hot chestnut; and *Dancing Kid,* where, under the impact of the bullets, the kid actually does dance as he dies —not to mention many others.

In these duels of speed, where the greased holster contends with one like an open box, as in *Johnny Concho,* the rule requires the adversaries to face each other. Only cowards shoot in the back, particularly when those they are aiming at have well-established reputations. Thus died Bill Hickok (*Wild Bill Hickok;* W. S. Hart, 1925), *The Plainsman, Buffalo Bill's Adventure* (Cecil B. DeMille, 1936) and Jesse James (*The Beloved Bandit, Jesse James,* Henry King, 1939). The essence of Otto Preminger's originality in *River of No Return* came from his tentative success in reinstating such a practice, though only in certain cases, of course.

In time, the Colt was modernized. From the "one shot" that in the classical period required raising the hammer after each shot (preferably with the left if one was right-handed), it became automatic, the barrel turned itself after each shot and the hammer recocked itself. James Cagney and his sons, the last examples of Texas feudalism, were so armed in one of Phil Karlson's last films. But this was not the only degeneration.

At the very time the Colt was standard, certain snobs,

for various reasons, used a small two-shot pistol, the Derringer. In *The Last Sunset* (Robert Aldrich, 1960), Kirk
Douglas used a similar weapon. As accurate as the Colt, it
was so light that it allowed one to be the fastest draw.
Equipped with a spring, a simple movement of the forearm
could make it pop out of the sleeve with the speed of lightning, to the great disadvantage of an opponent, outclassed
by mechanical progress (in *Texas Lady* and in Walsh's film).

A rival to the Colt, the semi-automatic rifle, whose lever
breech cleverly extends the trigger guard and permits a great
maneuvering speed, is the precision weapon par excellence. In
Vera Cruz (1954) Robert Aldrich tells how the Americans
bragged up their Winchesters to the Mexican emperor as
weapons which gave them formidable tactical superiority.
Buffalo Bill's Winchester, a one-in-a-million freak success,
has at this point become so legendary that an entire movie
was devoted to it. But *Winchester 75* by Anthony Mann is
not simply the history of the most beautiful gun in the world.
It contains the finest gunfight in film history. Traditionally,
the final battle in this type of film unfolds between the two
enemy brothers of this new Thebaide. In their plan of attack,
each exposes himself only to try to get the other while the
bullets ricochet off the rocks. Stephen McNally and James
Stewart, each in turn, crouch back into their crannies as the
bullets shatter the rocks, closer and closer to them.

The Winchester is so perfect an instrument that even today,
a century later, it is still in active use. It may be recognized,
in passing, in *The Lawless* (Joseph Losey, 1950) as well as,
in France, in Maurice Labo's *The Beast is Loose*.

The arrow, the spear, the tomahawk, the knife, the Colt,
the Derringer, the shotgun, and the rifle are not the only
Western weapons.

Beside the primitive machine gun of *Vera Cruz* (already

seen in the *Glorious Great Adventure* (Hathaway, 1939), it is necessary to point out a quite recent use of the rattle-snake, hooked to a long forked stick and thrown at the human target. This was the method used by Kirk Douglas' enemies in *The River of Our Love* (Andre de Toth) and he barely has time to cut the flying creature in two, with a shot. One of the heroes in *Cowboy* (Delmer Davis, 1958) is not so lucky. He dies by this weapon, used not in anger, but merely as a practical joke suited to the rough values of the cattle drivers.

War

The first World War saw the consecration of a new genre: the war film. However, perfection had already been attained episodically with the Civil War battle of Petersburg as Griffith created it in *Birth of a Nation* (1915), where the emphasis, as heavy on the horrible accumulation of corpses, as on heroism, was soon to become traditional in such spectacles. *Birth of a Nation* should not make one forget that in the preceding year Ince had turned out a *Battle of Gettysburg* with fewer resources but with even greater fecundity of invention. And then came the time of the heroes.

Just the titles of the films turned out by Pouctal from 1914 to 1918 tell the story without further discussion: *Alsace, The Girl of the Boche, Debt of Hate, The Nurse*. The same is true for the films of Poirier (*Verdun, Vision of History*) or of Gance (*Paddy's Heroism*) or a half-score others, all made under the supervision of Jean-Louis Croze, founder of the Cinematographic Service of the Army who, it is said, preserves in his warehouse dozens of miles of film shot at the front, and which, for obvious reasons, were never publicly shown save on rare, selected occasions, and which will not be seen again for some time.

The end of the war saw the reaction of pacifism in movie making. The most famous example is the ridiculous and grandiloquent *J'Accuse* (1919) of the turncoat Able Gance. The film did feature, however, a terrifying scene of killing around a water supply station, a parade of revived corpses, not a single one without a smashed face or a body that dangled flesh. Although spoiled by an excessive emphasis and a total lack of intelligence such prejudice can be beneficial. As witness the admirable *Heart of Spain* (Paul Strand, 1938). "In this film," recalls Ado Kyrou ("Surrealism in the Movies," p. 149) "is found a sequence which ranks among the most revolutionary in all cinema, because it confronts the viewer directly with his responsibilities, and forces him to take sides; therefore, to revolt. In the courtyard of a hospital, a nurse unwraps the bloody bandage which covers a stump; the wound soon appears in all its horror, and the average spectator gets ready to turn away his head or shut his eyes, but the commentary forces him to look by proclaiming: " 'Don't turn away, that is nonintervention!' " However, films which force one to take so close a look at the realities of war, and therefore to judge, are rare. The heaped bodies in the muck of the trenches in *The End of St. Petersburg* (Pudovkin, 1927), and the massacres of crowds by the police equated to the killing in a slaughterhouse (*The Strike,* Eisenstein, 1924) may be cited, but such scenes are barely suggested and sketchy in most films.

The American cinema, like the Soviet (apart from the period under Stalin), is however, among those which have shown the greatest courage in this area. *They Gave Him a Gun* (Van Kyck, 1937) and *All Quiet on the Western Front* (Lewis Milesone, 1930) remain quite unusual efforts, completely steeped in Rooseveltism. Belonging to the same school, although more recent, are *Take the High Ground* (Richard Brooks, 1953) where a man is killed simply because he stops to drink; *Men in War* (1956) where death absurdly looms up from the grass and flowers, as well as from the rubble and dust; *The Naked and the Dead* (Raoul Walsh), and *Between Heaven and Hell* (Richard Fleischer, 1956). These two last films are worth pausing over, since they represent current attitudes about war. In the first, a handsome figure of a sergeant, played by Aldo Ray sets fire to the grass with grenades in order to roast the enemy, and makes the prisoners —Japanese prisoners—die quickly. Not only does he take a certain pleasure in firing a machine gun at a mass of Japs, but after each skirmish even takes pliers from his pocket to pull out the corpses' gold teeth. In the second film, a homosexual commander, who has become half crazy with fear, transforms the place of his command into a gang hide-out.

Side by side with the condemning aspects, the same film offers at least two amazing exaltations of the military killer. The stages of the career of Hawkes' *Sergeant York* are retold in ("Positif" No. 11, p. 51): "a merry fellow who practices with his revolver instead of going to mass, one day receives a blow on the head, returns to the bosom of the church, joins the choir, and although a crackshot becomes a conscientious objector, then meets an understanding non-com who proves the necessity of defending civilization, does indeed defend it and finally, disdaining honors, retires like Cincinnatus." It is important to see the very well-directed scene where Gary Cooper, who plays York, goes beserk and, at a run, fires on everyone he sees in a German trench. The second World War also had its most highly decorated soldier, oddly enough, also the figure of a killer. Audie Murphy is a unique example of an actor who was hired by Hollywood because of his many decorations. Before becoming a rather bad Western hero, this character with the chubby face of a poorly-weaned choir boy played his own part in his own story. *To Hell and Back* (Jesse Hibbs) is involuntarily a rather extraordinary film in that it shows that Audie would have been incapable of killing had he not been brutally thrown into a state halfway between panicking terror and hysteria. He then becomes a veritable killing machine, made up entirely of blind reflexes of demented precision. Possibly the film served him (as was true of *I, A Negro*), as an autobiographical psychodrama, and relieved him of his strong neuroses? It is always shocking to see the contrast between the open face of this rejuvenated Mickey Rooney and the destructive rage which overcomes it.

A war hero's war hero is perhaps *A Real Man* (Stolper, 1938).

The influence of these war movies, even those made with the best of intentions, is surprising. In his book "This is the Movies," Georges Altman tells of a children's showing of "the strongest, most beautiful" of war films: *Four of the Infantry* (Pabst, 1930): the breathless kids followed it intensely, as if each battle were a big game . . . they looked for the actors of the drama, the strongest, and the weakest, the struggle and the victory. Suddenly, disaster for the French who crawl and spring and hurl themselves at command, and as suddenly, the cries of the children, viciously hurling themselves from the theater's darkness towards the terrible daylight of the screen.

"Go on! Go on! Kill 'em, yay French!"

THE KILLER

If violent death is as old as the history of the movies, then of necessity the same must be true for other than the military killer. The first Westerns, like the first thrillers, hardly emphasized the pathological pleasure that develops in those who kill or, even more, who make killing a profession.

The origin of this pleasure and its nature vary considerably according to genre.

The Western killer is foremost a technician. He knows how to use weapons better than the others. According to this principle, it matters little whether he is an outlaw, or, on the contrary, has, as marshal, the astuteness to put his virtuosity at the service of society, which pays better than the risky attacks on banks and stagecoaches. Roger Tailleur notes in "Positif" (No. 22) that the Western recognizes a social organization of crime, more or less legalized and far surpassing in its concept the bands organized by Billy the Kid or Mutch Cassidy, and he adds: "the man with the gun who lives by his weapon also dies by it: gunslinger, gunfighter or gunman, he follows a zigzag route along the thin line of the law, at one time serving it, at another against it". Therefore what is surprising if in *Wichita* (Jacques Tourneur) "the two men who have been paid to assassinate Wyatt Earp fall into his arms; they are his brothers."

The list of Western killers is long. They include: Buffalo Bill (*The Plainsman, Buffalo Bill's Adventure*, Cecil B. DeMille; *Buffalo Bill's Life*, P. Panzer, 1907; *Buffalo Bill*, William Wellman, 1944), Bill Hickok (*The Plainsman, Wild Bill Hickok*), *Billy the Kid* (King Vidor, 1930; Kurt Newman, 1947), Doc Holliday (*The Outlaw; My Darling Clementine*, Ford; *Gunfight at O.K. Corral*, John Sturges), Jesse James (Henry King, 1939; Nicholas Ray, 1956), Frank James (*The Return of Frank James*, Lang, 1940), the Daltons (*Gunfight at O.K. Corral; My Darling Clementine*) Johnny Ringo (*The Human Target*), etc.

To be skilful with a revolver does not make one less a man. The gunman may therefore be an intellectual (Frank James; the killer of *Star in the Dust,* Charles Hess), disillusioned (*Shane*), or to feel madness lies in wait. In *Johnny Guitar* (Nicholas Ray), Sterling Hayden doesn't want to touch a gun, since he knows that in his hand it will take on a mysterious life of its own, uncontrollably and terribly murderous. Finally, the killer of the Westerns possibly, is, or, always finds himself alone. Roger Tailleur continues: "the killer makes a void around himself; Sterling Hayden's wife abandons him in *Shotgun* and Jan Sterling does the same to Robert Mitchum in *Man With a Gun;* Rory Calhoun drives away Colleen Miller in *Four Killers and a Girl* so that she wouldn't have to share his perpetual flight; and in *Red Sundown* (Jack Arnold), Martha Hyer refuses to believe that the same Rory Calhoun has sincerely reformed. The former gunman, Glenn Ford, believed he had buried the past in *The Fastest Gun Alive* but this title so disturbs Broderick Crawford that he must challenge him for it. Loneliness and the unnatural quickness of reflexes throws the killer out of gear mentally, as it throws out Johnny Guitar. Usually, at the end of the film he goes off as he came, alone, alive, but for how long? ("Positif", No. 22, p. 22).

However, even in the most complex cases, during the worst see-sawing of emotional conflict, the Western hero never loses his romantic aura. The killer in thrillers is a completely different type, whose wholesomeness is utterly destroyed.

However, the debut of the gangsters was not so black. The exciting but unemotional supermen of *Chicago Nights* killed cleanly and without much relish. The murderous rage of *Scarface* was only a reflection of his wish for power. Sophistication actually arrived only in the forties, or rather, a little before, on a date that is the key to the American cinema: 1937. The pure assassin of *Gun Crazy* (Joseph H. Lewis, 1950), survives only as a stranger in a new world, because he is faithful to the old ethic.

Concurrently with this metamorphosis, several actors arise to stardom. Richard Widmark in *Kiss of Death* (Hathaway, 1947), creates a perpetually sneering character, the neurotic of dancehall and bar, whose presence is incomparably superior to the archetype of the soft hero, Victor Mature. Widmark made his name by his completely individual way of killing old ladies. He neatly ties them to their wheelchairs and shoves chair and occupant tumbling down a full flight of stairs. *In The Street With No Name* (William Keighley, 1948), as the toughest gangster among the toughs, he clears his head with a large shot of cocaine, and is so afraid of catching cold that he can not bear to have an open door at his back. His new fame arose from the contrast between this apparent weakness and the inexorable coldness of his murderous plans. Above all, the killer should be cold with a sharp lucidity (hence the use of cocaine) and, above all, should not lose his nerve. Shots are discouraged—too crude. It is now the reign of the ice-pick, fitted with a cap to cover the point. At the extreme, we come to *Murder by Contract* in which the hero, the American ideal of a young man copied from Gerald Norton, Ken Bald and Jerry Bronfield, has all the qualities, efficiency and self possession, professional awareness and a sporting sense—the young executive ideal. But returning to weapons, in *The Enforcer* (Bretaigne Windust, 1950) the efficiently used rifle is equipped with a telescopic lens and thus counts as a precision instrument. Otherwise this is the technique: the killers corner their victim in a barbershop just when he is blinded by a hot towel, gently push aside the terrified and dumbstruck barber, take his place and his razor, which they continue to sharpen gently for a completely different purpose.

The hysterical killers who live in a sort of perpetual rage gradually went out of style. The James Cagney of *White Heat* (Gordon Douglas, 1949) or *Kiss Tomorrow Goodbye* (1950, by the same director) maniacally pulling the trigger, is obviously dated in contrast to Raymond Burr, who in one episode kills his wife and cuts her up in the bathtub (*Rear Window,* Alfred Hitchcok, 1954), but who had started his career under better auspices before he began to go in for such an ordinary, actually so banal a crime. In an article in "L'Age du Cinema" (No. 2, p. 33), Ladilas Robin thus paints his portrait: "Raymond Burr made his entrance under the soft felt hat of the killer, cloaked in the impenetrable anonymity of the black novel. It is easier to enter this type of role than to leave it. However, from the time of *Red Light* (Rey del Ruth, 1949), his disturbing personality shaded into a new concept: Burr did not deign to shoot the big-mouth witness to his dealings. He waited until he took refuge in a garage under an enormous truck undergoing repairs. With one sufficient kick he knocks away the jack holding two tons in precarious balance, and coolly lets his victim be crushed into an inelegant pancake."

Such completely gratuitous cruelty was henceforth to be his trademark. In his latest films *Marketplace of Brutes,* Burr established something of a record; he has already treacherously burned several of his partners on the chest with his casual cigarette, impaled a rival with an antler, and disfigured a blonde dancer with a flaming bowl of punch. For him, anything that permits him to transcend the conventional brawls and kiss-offs, and to deal more than just one foul blow, is good.

Other new look killers include: Dan Duryea, specialist of

the frozen sneer in *Crisscross* (Robert Siodmak, 1949), *Blank Angel* (Roy William Neill, 1946), *Manhandled* (Lewis R. Foster, 1949) and *One Way Street;* and Richard Conte in *Call Northside 777* (Henry Hathaway, 1947), *Cry of the City,* (Robert Siodmak, 1948) and *Somewhere in the Night* (Joseph L. Mankiewitz, 1946), whose apparent graciousness hides a treasurehouse of criminal stubbornness. There is Ernest Borgnine, made evil by the very weight of his physical ugliness, in *The Mob* (Robert Parrish, 1951). And the Shakespearean Jack Palance in *Panic in the Street* (Elia Kazan, 1950), and in *Sudden Fear* (David Miller, 1952). And Lee Marvin who also has Burr's skillful technique with a lighted cigarette and boiling liquid in *The Big Heat* (Fritz Lang, 1955). And, without ending the list, there is Ralph Meeker in *Jeopardy* (John Sturges, 1952) and *Kiss Me Deadly* (Robert Aldrich, 1957) to which we'll come back.

A GLOSSARY OF THE LESS COMMONPLACE DEATHS

This is a discussion of means of killing other than by cold steel, whether scissors as in *The Lady in the Portrait, The Almost Perfect Crime,* or of firearms from the harquebus to the P38. Killers and destiny are very inventive. Here is an alphabetical catalog of fourteen of these novelties—the most outstanding.

Asphixiation: One of my first cinematographic memories, an anonymous one, is a classic episode of the serial. The hero finds himself shut in a hermetically sealed room, and suddenly the sinister hiss of lethal gas is heard. Less ambitiously, a new version of the famous episode occurs in *Fantomas* (Louis Feuillade, 1913-14); the wealthy guests at an evening party suddenly notice that the ballroom windows are walled up; they are killed by gas, and the thieves have only to gather their plunder of jewels from the corpses. Among other virtues, *We're No Angels* (William Keighley) is famous for an ingenious infernal machine which Calder could have designed, its purpose being to let drop a very fragile glass sphere filled with noxious fumes. Less concerned with esthetics, Justice lacks these prettinesses. The death of Red Babs in the gas chamber of San Quentin is prepared with meticulous detail by qualified workers, *I Want to Live* (Robert Wise); and if they are preoccupied with spreading a carpet for the bare feet of the condemned, it is only their "humanity" trying to pacify their conscience after the horror. *Lethal Gas* (Able Gance, 1916) was martial rather than criminal, from the days, before the atomic bomb, when gas was the number one secret weapon.

Asphixiation from lack of air is the sister of poisoning the atmosphere, the leif motif of stories about deep-sea divers from *Twenty Thousand Leagues Under The Sea* (from the MacCutcheon to the Richard Fleischer version) to *Nitchevo* to *S. O. S. 103* by Commandant Francisco de Robertis. Even more recently, a quite extraordinary document, although spoiled by a stupid montage meant to be dramatic, was shown to us. Trapped in a German submarine leaking from a torpedo hit, one of the sailors made a film of the crew's agonies that ended with the death of the operator himself. The film was recovered when the U-boat floated to the surface. It splendidly fulfills its promise.

Before leaving death from lack of air, thought should be given to the countless actors who drowned in film history, to Paul Muni, who in the cabin of a sinking ship *Souls of the Sea* (Hathaway), less fortunate than Dorothy Malone is later, cannot free himself; recall also the poetic drowned girl, her long hair floating, in *The Night of the Hunter* (Charles Laughton), the cinematic relative of all the Ophelias.

The Atom: In our society the progress of civilization coincides perfectly with improved means of killing. TNT having been invented in the Nineteenth Century, the Twentieth discovered the atomic bomb and a new type of death, uniting the charms of explosion with the attractions of radioactivity. The first victims of radiation were *Mr. and Mrs. Curie* whose admirable story was poetically told by Georges Franju. But today's victims no longer have the bitterness of their death compensated by the joys of discovery.

The Dantesque *Hiroshima* (Hideo Sekigawa) leads us in long journeys across a haunting city of cinders, charred beams and melted girders, where the mangled bodies of the inhabitants lie twisted. Several years pass but the *Children of Hiroshima* (Kanato Shindo) continue to die in silence, filled with Christian resignation, while the fishermen, who had ventured too close to Bikini, show the newsreels their faces devoured by cankers; and that despite all this, oblivion aided by literature, begins to cover the ruins collected by the museums (*Hiroshima, Mon Amour;* Alain Resnais). Fear alone remains, for this mysterious and enormous power which is locked in Pandora's box in *Kiss Me Deadly.*

As belles lettres and myth testify, fantasy has recourse to the atom. Atomic explosions route out the monsters from the depths of the sea (*The Monster from the Past,* Eugene Lourie) when radiation is not increasing the size of ants of New Mexico a hundredfold (*Them*). The monstrous *Godzilla* destroys cities, thanks to his radioactive breath.The A-bomb stands aside only in the face of *The Power from on High.* In *The War of the Worlds* (Bryon Haskin) the nuclear weapon is useless against the Martians, but more fortunately than in Ridgeway's version, terrestrial microbes gain God's victory.

Cataclysm: The strong predilection for atomic catastrophe

is only the final stage of an old taste for cataclysm. Since the day when Meleas reenacted the eruption of Mount Pelle, the geography of the movies is rich with violences of all types. Let us pity the hurtling crowds of the *Last Days of Pompei* (Ernest Shoedsack, then Mario Bonnard) and Ingrid Bergman, solitary among the fumes of *Stromboli*. Volcanoes are a favorite dressing for adventure; they furnish climaxes as magnificent as one could wish to the serial *Jungle Jim*. Great conflagrations provide a natural alternative, in the different versions of *Quo Vadis, Carthage in Flames* (Carmine Callone), and *The Chicago Fire*. (Henry King).

Here, water does not fight fire but assists it. The broken barrier in *The Monsoon* (Clarence Brown) foretells Malpasset's newsreel. In the two versions of *The Ten Commandments* of fire, if one may say so, by Cecil B. DeMille, the Red Sea engulfs the impious army of Pharoah.

Cremation: When less spectacular, fires are not less cruel, and are possibly more so because the accent is on the agony of burning rather than on the esthetics of flame. Women die in burning theatres, *Sweet* (Claude Autant-Lara), or in blazing mansions, *Rebecca* (Alfred Hitchcock), but men often prefer gasoline, *A Man is Finished* (John Sturges) or in methane tanks, *White Heat; Odds Against Tomorrow* (Wise).

Finally, fire as torture. Apart from several versions of Moloch and Baal, *Cabiria* (Pastrone); *Carthage in Flames* (Callone), the various Salambos, planned cremation is even the favorite Christian tool of purification. Many witches have been burned on the screen. Joan of Arc is the most illustrious, and neither Dreyer nor Victor Fleming, advised by the clergy, favored us with a single log or curl of smoke. The same Dreyer in his *Dies Irae* consumed a less well-known fiend, but added a choice soundtrack; the crackling of the flames are balanced by the angelic voices of the tiny choir children. Less concerned with pure beauty, Ingmar Bergman dwelt on the horror of torture. *The Seventh Seal* shows in detail the victim martyred by the priests, who are apparently more concerned with obtaining rare pleasures than upholding the Lord. In Rene Clair's *My Wife is a Witch,* Veronica Lake and her sorcerer father are burned at a less tragic stake. Optimistically, the same film also proves that he who perishes by fire shall be reborn by fire, and that Satan, in this supreme instant, does not always abandon his creatures. He causes storms whose rain extinguishes the blazing logs, *The Mask of the Demon* (Mario Bava).

Let us be fair, churches, pagan or Christian, do not have exclusive rights to torture by burning. It is not through them that the heroine of *Blazing Mass of Silver* (Volkov) and the pioneers in *Drums Along The Mohawk* died; the latter tied on haycarts ignited by the Indians' flaming arrows.

More sombrely, we must refer to the victims of the furnaces in the death camps. An American film clip, that has never been exhibited again since the early days of the liberation, because it was judged too violent for calm consciousnesses, shows a G.I. opening the door of an oven and pulling out the twisted corpse of a half-consumed "subhuman". Another scene reveals a body converted by a flame-throwing machine into a horrible and fragile statue of cinders.

The war film has also discovered the power of fire. *Okinawa* (Milestone) and many others leave the job largely to portable or motorized flame-spitting machines. More primitive, but also effective are Aldo Ray's methods in *The Naked and the Dead,* previously cited.

Crucifixion: This is the most famous torture in the world, considering the importance of the sufferer, a minor Sicilian official who Verres, ancestor of the Mafia, ordered crucified, cf. Cicero, "De Suppliciis". Crucifixion soon had its hour of glory in the movies, with another hero it is true (but producers, as everyone knows, are devoid of general culture), a Galilean named Jesus. *The Passion* (Zecca and Nonguet) opened in 1903 with incomparable assurance in the void of the worst Saint-Sulpicerie. The subject, popularized by a publicity campaign which had been in operation for about nineteen centuries, brought in a lot of money. This has been repeatedly remade with great Swiftian success. Before Zecca's version there was *The Passion* by Lear (no relation to Edward Lear), then those by Holaman, Sigmund Lubin, and even, currently, *The Robe* (Koster), *Barabas* (Sjoberg), better inspired by Strindberg and, to finish a very fragmentary list, the agony of the Christians in *Slaves of Carthage,* where following the tradition of Nero, as delineated in *Nero and Agrippina* (Caserine), the victims are not only crucified, but also set on fire.

Crushing: In high gear, keeping the eye trained on *Red Light* (Roy del Ruth) shows how to liquidate a witness as he is kneeling to repair a truck. Just remove the jack. In *Border Incident,* Anthony Mann perfects this technique, replacing the relatively elastic tires by the firmer caterpillar treads of a bulldozer in order to squash a recalcitrant Mexican worker. It is still caterpillar treads, but this time on a military vehicle which *Comrade P* (Ermler) uses to satisfy a justified vengeance by executing the SS who had killed his child. At command, a swift tank brings him to bay against a wall of rock, and thrusts its engine against him. The camera, by preceding the tank, permits us to savor, to the bitter end, the just execution of a Nazi.

Presses in general, and especially hydraulic presses, are used for crushing. Therefore, it is under a press that the convicts in *Demons of Liberty* (Jules Dassin), push the comrade who has betrayed them, as they threaten him with blowtorches. Dassin lets the film stop at the moment when the huge piston comes down on the body; but *The Fly* dwells on the action much longer. In "Sight and Sound", Derek Hill discusses it: *"The Fly* creates the repetition of a sequence of a body being crushed by a hydraulic press. The first time, we are shown the blood which trickles from the jaws of the press; the second time, we see the body writhe while the press descends on it." And Derek Hill carefully notes that the fact that the second sequence is cut just at that moment in order to show the victim's wife "appears to arise more from the difficulty of showing a body being crushed than by any consideration for the feelings of the viewer." For our part, we express only regret. This ravishing dispersion of hemoglobin has a very bad soundtrack, although it would have been so easy to have complemented the action with several well-chosen soft, slow, nauseating crunches.

Subtler than this industrial instrument are walls, made famous by Poe's *The Pit and the Pendulum,* walls which slowly come together to crush the prisoner. We will find them again in *The Raven* (Louis Freilander) and in *The Golden Mask* (Charles Brabin).

Decapitation: The film history of the guillotine is as long, or almost as long, as that of Christ. If Dr. Frankenstein, the petty atheist, succeeds in having the prison chaplain executed in his stead, in *The Revenge of Frankenstein* (Terence Fisher), if Fantomas, aided by Feuillade, delivers over to the knife an actor whom he resembles like a brother, less fortunate are the innumerable decapitated souls in films of the French revolution, that was the work of drunkards and assassins, as every moron knows. From *Madame du Barry* (Lubitsch, 1919) to the sinister *Marie Antoinette* by our fellow countryman Delannoy, and including *Pages Torn From the Book of*

Satan (1921) by the inevitable Dreyer, many heads rolled, cut off while the rabble hooted. In Dreyer's film, the terrifying revolutionaries pushed cruelty and cynicism to the extent of installing their machine in the court of the manor lord they were about to execute.

The guillotine also served less just causes. It is towards it that *Monsieur Verdoux* is led, and to which Julien Sorel climbs in *The Red and the Black* (Claude Autant-Lara, 1954). Again, it is the old girl herself who stresses her menace throughout the boring *We Are All Murderers* (Cayatte) and who provides the sinister end in the *Golden Casket* (Becker).

This invention of the good Dr. Guillotine was the object of admirable journalism. To reveal the full horror of *A Capital Execution,* Lucien Hayer hid himself in the washroom of a prison and was able to film the ceremony of decapitation as it took place in the courtyard.

Finally, the guillotine is not the only weapon for chopping off heads. From *Anne Boleyn* (Lubitsch) to *Elizabeth and Essex* (Michael Curtiz) where Errol Flynn dies at Bette Davis' command, it is proved that the sword and the axe had their use. The only hope is that the head will not continue to live by itself like that of the sorcerer in the *Headless Man,* the dogs in *The Mechanism of the Brain* or like the bloated face of Michel Simon scientifically nourished in *The Naked and the Devil* (1959).

Electrocution: Electrocution, like the guillotine, generally serves to execute criminals or alleged criminals. It thus appears suddenly at the end of countless thrillers, *Red Light* for example, or, even better, *Angels with Dirty Faces* where James Cagney, heroically frightened, dies a coward. Sometimes in horror movies the condemned are transformed into supermen through electrocution and escape (*The Escape from the Elec-*

tric Chair), endowed with remarkable powers. At other times, the fatal chair is a pretext for more or less happy gags as in *The Five Sous of Lavarede*.

The criminals are here more skillful than the officials. *Fantomas* electrocutes an entire circus. Even more inventive is the assassin in *The Last Warning* (Paul Leni, 1929) who connects with the main power line, the copper chandelier on stage, which an actor must seize.

Engulfment, Burial: The slow entombment of a living body which sinks deeper the more it struggles is possibly one of the most terrifying means of death. Often it is only a suspense scene, and the hero escapes this fate in the end; so it goes in *Wagon Train West* (Cruze) and in the many versions of *The Hound of the Baskervilles* (Sidney Landfield, 1939; Terence Fisher, 1958).

Less fortunate in their hand-to-hand struggles with quicksand are the Indian criminal in *The Adventures of Tom Sawyer,* the killer in *The Last of the Six* (George Lucombe) and an unfortunate member of the glorious Yankee cavalry corps who, in *Run of the Arrow* (Samuel Fuller), falls from a tree and is sucked down by the mire in a wink.

After citing the originality of *Christ in Concrete* where Edward Dmytryck replaces the traditional mud with concrete, let us mention a kindred style of death. This is the torture which consists of burying the victim up to the head and letting him be killed by hunger, or ferocious beasts. The many versions of *Michael Strogoff* each tell of this half-burial in their own way, but cannot make one forget the formal beauty in the shots of *Viva Mexico* where three Indians, buried up to the neck, are trampled on by horses and left to the appetite of the vultures.

Epidemic: If he is not the first, Murnau is the most important of those who portray the threat of death from disease.

Nosferatu brings the plague with him and, just as bacterial death walked in the vampire's tracks, it accompanies disease in general since, in *Faust,* the demon's shadow blends with the arrival of the deadly malady. A juggler ceases his performance to crumple up and die like an animal. A little later, charmingly quaint circus rigs enhance the contortions of the plague-stricken corpses.

The United States sacrifices the cruel and inhuman aspect of disease to the myth of the doctor, currently popularized in the novels of Frank Slaughter. *Jezebel* (William Wyler, 1938), as well as *Forever Amber* (Preminger), which recalls "Journal of the Plague Year" by Daniel Defoe, or *Arrowsmith* (1931) offer discreet and refined shots in which several drops of sweat on the brow of the dying person suffice to represent physical demise and the fear of death.

Less attractive to look at are the victims of cholera, vomiting their guts out in *The Proud and the Damned* or those of *Nazarin* where a priest tries to ruin the last moments of the dying. Less beautiful still, in a return to the cosmic terrors of Murnau, is the head with eyes eaten-out, by which the Black Death announces his entrance in *The Seventh Seal.*

Mastication: If jungle films call for many attacks by man-eating animals, cats, piranhas and red ants, it is rare that the feast itself is shown. The sacred crocodiles in *Toura, Goddess of the Jungle* are therefore among the fortunate reptiles, since one can see them snapping up their human prey with care; as do the swathed mummies, and the dogs in *The Eyes Without A Face* who, while less-favored, are privileged carnivores, being permitted to tear Pierre Brasseur into strips.

Monsters do not have to beg for these rare privileges. The great roc in *Sinbad the Sailor, The Monster of the Past* and other inhabitants of *Lost World* (Harry D. Hoydt) and *King Kong* (Ernest B. Schoedsack and Merian Cooper, 1933) can nourish themselves on human flesh with greater ease and freedom, their fantastic forms excusing the somewhat reprehensible nature of their appetite. Tyrannosaurs, dinosaurs and their more or less grown and advanced descendants have the lion's share of the feast. Eugene Lourie's monster is favored even among the privileged, since he is given a choice morsel to snap up, a policeman who can be seen squirming in his teeth.

Man is man's prey, as the poetic saying goes; let us not forget the cannibals. They are hardly ever missing from a Tarzan film or its equivalent; but whites who feed on human flesh are rarer. From the scraps left by the savages in *Robinson Crusoe* (Bunuel) let us turn to the peacemaker of *Northwest Passage* (King Vidor, 1940), who having become mad after being clouted by an Indian, keeps a human head in his soldier's pack, from which he crunches a little morsel each day. Equally abominable is the huge snowman of *The Conquest of the Pole* (Melies), a creature born of timber and packing-cases, and whose ingenious combination of pulleys permits him to seize venturesome explorers by their legs, and to put them delicately in the oven of his mouth. The Baal in *Cabiria* (Pastrone) was similarly concerned with little children who were sacrificed to him. From above it could be seen that he also had a white-hot mouth and a glowing gullet.

Are the Morlocks men, and is their ingestion of the Elois related to cannibalism? Are the Elois themselves, despite the fact they look it, men? Is this the ultimate form of the class struggle? These are the many questions raised by Wells, and which *The Time Machine* (George Pal, 1960) either cannot answer or refuses to resolve.

Plunge: The fall, followed by death, is the concern of the mountain film. From the pre-Nazi movies of Arnold Franck, exalting foolhardy exploits and gratuitous danger — seen particularly in *White Hell* — and *The Blue Light* (Bela Balazes) up to *First on Cordee* (Louis Daquin, 1944), *Annapurna, The First 8,000,* to similar Spencer Tracy films, men scale cliffs for the glory of it and sometimes suffer spectacular falls.

The terror of vertigo is combined with the horror of falling. It occurs on unprotected walls but also along cliffs and public monuments. Gregory Peck and Anthony Quinn in *The Guns of Navaronne* achieve a very difficult climb, handicapped by sea birds who dart out and startle them at the most perilous passages. Hitchcock is the master of drain pipes which give way (*Rear Window* 1954; *To Catch A Thief,* 1956) and sleeves, the only link that supports you in empty space, tear loose at the top of the Statue of Liberty (*Saboteur,* 1942). One step further and vertigo becomes metaphysical and gives its title to a film; in *Vertigo* (1958), the hero, as is understood, has a phobia about steeples. All this is only a minor matter and a pale copy of the raving lunatic *Safety Last* (acrophobe's hell!) and of its remake, with sound, *At The Top* where the hero, Harold Lloyd, by dint of delirious aerial feats along the wall of a skyscraper for a full hour succeeds in keeping the viewer in a state of complete weightlessness.

If you know how to fly, you also know how to fall. In keeping with this principle, the fall has been perfected and the aircraft has replaced natural heights and architectural masterpieces. The hero of *Master of the World* at the end of the film undergoes a vertiginous fall, with a parachute, from an airborne dirigible. Others jump from airplanes, but as they are equipped with parachutes, their fall to earth has only very feeble interest, from our point of view.

Interest revives only when the airplane falls with its pilot. The history of the aviation film is fertile with perilous tail-spins and fatal nose-dives. Let us cite the versions of *Dawn*

Patrol (Hawks, 1930; Edmund Golding, 1938), *Fog* (1935) and *Only Angels Have Wings* (1939), both by Hawks. The last war has so multiplied the airborn epics that even to list the accidents would be tedious. But it is worth mentioning an admirable but little-known film *The Flying Men* (Wellman, 1939) made prior to the war, and in which the brave, twin-engine craft marvelously tells the story of flying. The hazards of those days permit the director to make his hero perish when he crashes and the fuel tank explodes. The film was in color, and the plane could be seen rolling over and over, engulfed in red flames, on a golden field of wheat.

Sawing: Within the confines of a mechanized sawmill, that usually processes tree trunks into planks; the heroine is tied to the moving belt; and finds herself slowly pulled towards a circular saw. Meanwhile the hero is racing to her, but finds himself still too far away, exposed to so many ambushes that he does not know if he will arrive in time. This situation has spiced countless episodes of the serials from *The Perils of Pauline* (Louis Gasnier, 1914) to the more modern *G-Men Against the Black Dragon*. One Mack Sennett film even parodies this very terrifying situation. Because the rescuer has not arrived in time, the belt moves back to give the necessary extra time.

Strangulation, Hanging: Accidental strangulation knows no better than operate with the aid of a long scarf and a "vintage car". The scarf wraps itself around the axle and the owner, in a last reflex, raises her arms to her throat in vain. Such was the death of Isadora Duncan which Melville used in his adaptation of *Les Enfants Terribles* by Cocteau. Strangulation of criminals is the privilege of Asia. Some heroes of the Italian Renaissance attempted to try it in *Lucretia Borgia* (Abel Gance, 1935), but in comparison with the terrifying organization of Hindu sects, they were strictly amateurs. The last homage rendered to the knights of the silken cord is *Strangler of Bombay* (Terence Fisher, 1959) a British film, as it should be.

The hanged are the brothers of the strangled. The hanged man coated with tar in *He Who Laughs* (Paul Muni) is possibly the one discovered by the terrified young hero of *Moonfleet* (Fritz Lang). At least they both had the advantage of comparative physical integrity, while the unfortunate clients of the gallows in *Captain Fracasse,* with whom Gance's hero collides, are reduced to nothing more than shreds of flesh hanging on vestiges of shocking skeletons.

DEATH IN PERSON

When he is incarnated, Death is, for the most part, not very horrible. He takes care not to inspire terror. His appearance in *Hilde Warren and Death* (Joe May, from a scenario by Fritz Lang, 1918), praised in "The General History of the Cinema" by Georges Sadoul (Vol. 3, 2 pl. 119), is rather exceptional.

The first of the personifications was the tall black silhouette of Death in *Three Lights* (1921). Lotte Eisner writes: "The silent films of Lang, as also the scenario writer for Rippert, show us several variations on the theme of death, vibrating in a minor key; it is the leit motif of *Three Lights*, called in German, *Der Mude Tod, (Weary Death)*. Within the frame of the principal story, that of a young woman who wishes to snatch her lover from Death, three episodes, unfolding in different periods are merely variations with identical endings. All the girl's efforts to save her beloved lead him to his ruin." ("Demonic Screen," p. 45-45.) Death, who knows that he is inevitable, has the inexorable sweetness of logical reasoning. The knight of *The Seventh Seal,* is therefore all the more courageous in matching his strength in a game with his black-hooded skin-clad opponent. He knows beforehand that he will lose the game, but despite that he plays to prove that the honor of his being human lies in not accepting that which turns life into fate.

Death, borrowing the body of his latest victim, can operate for a whole year (*The Phantom* Cart, Sjostrom, 1920) until the twelfth stroke of midnight on December 31 dispossesses him. In the talkie remake (Duvivier, 1938), as Louis Jouvet he has the pleasure of threatening Pierre Fresnay. He can also put to flight a bus or hold the reins of a horse-drawn hearse in *Dead Of Night* (Hamer, Crichton, Deardon and Cavalcanti, 1945). Finally, he can, in the guise of the elegant Prince Sirki (Frederic March), spend some time in Italy (*Death Takes A Holiday,* Mitchell Leisen). He is always without passion, without anger, strong in his immutable reason.

His apparent set-backs are only temporary, strategic checks. Those were seen in the *Seventh Seal*. They can also be seen in **Heaven Can Wait** (Lubitsch, 1943) as well as in *Six Hours To Live* (William Dieterle) where, revived for six hours by Professor Bauer's machine, Captain Onslow can devote himself to a final and surpassingly elegant earthly stroll. If death does blunder, he is never at a loss in finding bodies to replace, temporarily, the victims of such errors *Here Comes Mr. Jordan* (Alexander Hall). If, finally, someone tricks him up a magic tree from which it is impossible to climb down, this bad joke, when played by Lionel Barrymore, quickly reveals Death as sort of minor official, necessary to the smooth functioning of the world, eternal comforter that he is. This is the debatable moral of Harold Bucquet's *Strange Reprieve*.

Busy as he is off-stage, Death nonetheless has a romantic aura in several admirable films. Without referring to the countless and often engaging ghost movies in cinematic history, ignoring the painters of the naive afterworld in *Green Pastures* (William Keighley), and particularly Minnelli's Hell in *Cabin in the Sky*, it is still necessary to mention *Voyage of No Return* (Tay Garnett) where the situation rises from a fatal lyricism. The man and the woman loving each other, know they are both condemned. In "Love, Eroticism and the Movies", Ado Kyrou tells their story: "A man (William Powell) and a woman (Kay Francis) meet on an ocean liner travelling from Shanghai to San Francisco. He is an adventurer, condemned to death; a policeman is taking him back to the United States where the electric chair awaits him. She is also going to an inexorable end: the doctors have definitely condemned her. The crossing, that lasts eighteen days, will be the span of their love. Each is conscious of being condemned, but the word 'death' does not dim this mad love (p. 395)."

One knows of no better way to finish with death.

MORALITY

When, in the name of burlesque, Calino or Cretinetti's limbs are gaily torn off, nothing in the film is felt to be offensive. The authors of such films were hardly concerned with morality. After the second World War, times changed and nowadays violence calls for reflection and judgment.

To each master, his due. The American cinema, which appropriated for itself the biggest segments of blows, wounds and diverse deaths, should draw the best lessons from its experience. Three filmmakers specially undertook this job: Robert Aldrich, Richard Brooks and Anthony Mann.

Aldrich, Brooks, Mann

As Plutarch, who never lacked a maxim, said in reference to the education of children: "the two principal attributes of human nature are intelligence and reason." Therefore, some directors, more honorable than others, are not content merely to describe by portraying brutality but undertake to examine its in and outs, its reasons and motivations, its ends and means.

Anthony Mann is possibly the best example of this approach. Producer of black films, Raymond Burr's director during the period of his little chores, discovered one lovely

71

morning, in *The Devil's Doorway* (1950), by the luck of
a Western that just hit on it, what he had already glimpsed in
Border Incident. The victory of rage and force is always the
vilest. It becomes for example, the most common element in
racism. The Western always helping, he invented in the guise
of James Stewart, a thorough-going hero who at every instant
is blinded by a murderous rage but who always has the courage
to restrain his fury. Betrayed and knocked about by his
brother (*Winchester 75*), abandoned on a mountain (*The
Hungry Ones*), fearfully wounded in the hand and dragged
through the dust (*The Plainsman*), flouted by a cynical judge
(*I Am An Adventurer*) he inevitably feels a tremor of literally
mad fury, which brings the glint of murder to his eye. But he
always manages to stop in time and at the last moment re-
frains from yielding to that passion, which in a flash of
lucidity, he realizes makes him as despicable as his adversaries.
Holding Arthur Kennedy at gunpoint he will not kill him,
despite all his justifications. For this hero, justice is only
justice when it is calm and impassive.

In the single Western that he produced, Richard Brooks
was moved by similar concerns, possibly more systematically
organized, but just as earnest. Robert Taylor who kills Indians
and buffalo for fun, literally shooting like a madman, his rifle
resting against his shoulder and symbolically pointed ahead,
and who works over Russ Hamblyn to calm his nerves and
appease his remorse, is equivalent to Stewart Granger who
is moved by the same taste for killing and brawling but who
knows, miraculously, how to stop in time, on the verge of
shameful or neurotic behavior. *The Last Hunt* comes at the
end of a long series of films. "In *Key Largo,* Bogart triumphs
by a trick, but more to save his life than to defeat justice,
for which he has no concern; and as even with the necessary
death of others, a mild disgust is always mixed with his vic-

tory, an executioner in spite of himself, who needs only the eyes of the waiting Lauren Bacall to expunge his disgust." wrote Louis Sequin ("Positif" No. 17 p. 12). And he adds: "this distrust of rapture which they say seeks the scent of powder leads the author of *Crisis* to the verge of a relatively suspect ambiguity; starting with the exaltation of flames on a deserted spot and a decaptitated statue, the revolution ends in pillage, assassination and cynicism." The indispensable distinctions will be made only much later, when they examine the reasons for the use of violence after the journey to the edge of night in *Take The High Ground,* where for want of having read Clausewitz, Sergeant Ryan searches in vain for an internal logic of war.

And *Blackboard Jungle* can finally distinguish between the brutality Glenn Ford learned in knocking a student down, and the crafty savagery of Vic Morrow who, in order to be sure of himself, must carry a knife.

In one of Robert Aldrich's first films (still a Western), violence is more directly linked to the prestige of virility. Massai, the rebel Indian (Burt Lancaster), treats his future wife like a slave, or even worse, inflicts token pain thus assuring himself of his own strength, and of his glorious qualities as man and warrior. He understands only afterwards that the opposite, tenderness, is a more appropriate course. All Aldrich's female characters are cast in the same mold. Usually tender up to their actual villainy, as witness Marian Carr, Martine Carol, Santa Montiel, and Ida Lupino, all are fickle, all victims of aggression, because at contact with them, violence works itself to death, loses its strength, and finds itself deprived of its nourishment, which is anger and blind impetuosity, naked and despicable.

If one considers *Kiss Me Deadly* and *Attack* as the two poles of Aldrich's morality, it is because they both denounce the inanity of brute force, effected in the first by the absurd, and in the second by a spiralling exaggeration of his philosophy.

Kiss Me Deadly is, as has often been noted, the most complete version of the black film because it is the most frenetic. Mike Hammer, Mickey Spillane's precious hero, wanders among the dreary evidences of roving, unpausing cruelty which jumps from a young woman who is tortured, to a garage-hand crushed by the method used in *Red Light*. To this madness, he can respond only with even more terrible madness, a beast more savage than the beasts with whom he contends. Violence leading to violence, this perpetual inflation spirals to an outcome as mad as it is natural: the end of the world in a blaze of an atomic explosion. This folly is all the more perfect since it knows how to avoid death sometimes, then let it rise to the surface again, after which the madness is all the more discernible. Such is the tender devotion of Marian Carr. Aldrich's nihilism is as vehement as his affirmation, a nihilism of method.

Attack is to the war film what *Kiss Me Deadly* is to the thriller, an overstimulated variation, an engine strained to the point where one wonders if it can finish the course. It does finish it. Linked to the play on which it is based, this film tells of the villainy and moral condemnation of an evil officer, but is specially designed to come to a mathematically precise end with the calvary of Jack Palance; his arm crushed, this bloody, mud-covered, howling, crawling man drags himself along a wall, with, instead of an arm, a mere scrap trickling blood at the shoulder.

It is not a coincidence that Aldrich's heroes are played by experts in the role of killers: Dan Duryea in *Danger in Singapore*, Ralph Meeker in *Kiss Me Deadly*, and finally Jack Palance in the *Big Knife, Attack,* and *The Phoenix.* It is fitting to lead these handsome faces of bloody heroes to their very end, to the zero point where they lose themselves or annihilate themselves. If Anthony Mann learned to distrust violence, if Brooks had found its causes, it belongs to the last of the three, Robert Aldrich, to show how it should burn in its own flame, break by the force of its own absurdity. Finally, it is symptomatic that once this description, this lesson and this method are exposed, our three authors find themselves, surprisingly, at first glance, but, on reflection, logically, at the end of their respective inspirations.

After *Hill 465* where the Korean War is seen by the reflected light of the Western, Anthony Mann with a *Cimaroon,* a strange figure of an insatiable adventurer, whose behavior would, however, have been wondrous to describe, took pleasure in a picturesque experiment in a gifted style; but these could not compete with the seriousness of his old preoccupations. Having become famous and respected as an intellectual producer, Brooks shifted brutally, with suspicious frenzy, to neo-realism and, worse still, adopted Tennessee Williams. Aldrich, after various biblical adventures, finally failed to find in *The Last Sunset* the sun-scorched paradise of his first love affair with the West.

DESIRE AND CRUELTY

While the movies offer all conceivable variations on violence or, better, on death, they always do their utmost to purify the rationale of these exhibitions. It is unwholesome to show the homosexual of *Fireworks* set upon by the sailors, but it is healthy to show Humphrey Bogart or Alan Ladd soaking up a more than sufficient ration of punches or black-jack blows. The motives acknowledged by Kenneth Anger are of a sexual nature, as others dare not. The narrative speaks of justice, of country; never of desire. On the one hand there is morality, on the other there is not.

Of course no one is fooled; neither the producers, nor the distributors; nor the directors; nor the public; nor even the censor. Any one, I repeat anyone, who applauds the punches Rock Hudson gives and takes in *Giant* (George Stevens, 1956), in that famous scene, must confess that these cheers are not simply to reward or admire the antiracism of the hero, nor the charm of the (in fact) vulgar setting. In short the most apt, like the most superfluous punches, the most casual wounds and the most natural deaths are alike subject to the psychological interpretation of he who invents, executes or watches them. The censor is so well aware of this that he is beginning to track down violence with the same standards that he hunts down sex; that is, with the same ardor and dishonesty, since violence is always, or nearly always, when it is represented in a manner that carries conviction, a display of dedication — I mean of earnest, effective sincerity.

But the movies have not taken the long-range view in this. They, too, exploit each favorable opportunity to paint with a little less prudence, and in a more detailed fashion, certain deviations of taste where, thanks to the opulence of its methods and the sophistication of its setting, cruelty is rediscovered, magnified, and blended with desire.

RAPE

THE WHIP

TORTURE

Before beginning the fetishistic parade of situations and instruments, it is necessary to tarry at the point where cruelty and desire are most elementally united — rape, resulting from sheer need, or, better still, from appetite. All else will then follow the more naturally; as is true of all developed thought, the first requirement is a solid foundation.

At least, Aristotle more or less assures us of this.

RAPE

Villiers' hero on the "Isle of Adam," shrewdly comments: "You say that in Paris, the young girls, the children *do not cry?* . . . Ah, it is exactly of this that various connoisseurs, and we among them, complain! . . . Consider the birdbrain French! Because they take a few innocent liberties, play some children's games, are granted some banal favors, note that they believe themselves to be princes of debauchery! In truth, we are more . . . serious" ("Histoires Insolites").

This fundamental principle of sadism, that the non-consent of the love object is the most primitive requirement, even the primary one, is validated by rape. The movies grasp this, just like Villiers' character, and consequently appear more "serious". But they always need alibis; as much because of their authors' own timidity as because of social strictness, they cover up the rapes they depict by pretexts of varying artistic value and of limited range, although these pretexts are sometimes used in combination. These pretexts are: peasant life; religion; military life; social inequality; and the world of crime.

The painting of rural mores is never free from uncouthness. Farm girls are never courted, save when they are forced. That, apparently, is nature's law. That's the way both Charles Vanle in *The Farm of the Hanged* (Jean Drevilles, 1946) and the peasant who became lustful at the sight of Bernadette Lafond in *Beau Serge* (Claud Chabrol, 1958) act. The citations are not meant as praise, since their authors behave with complete lack of imagination, without refinement. Rape, which never occurs without utter alcoholic befuddlement, hereditary or otherwise, is the result of an elementary burgeoning of brutality, and this primal state is portrayed as if the subject were fading and the painter was abashed that the narration concerns a theme lacking in properly polished elegant interest.

Its ingenuity and richness begin with history, especially with the history of the Middle Ages and the Renaissance. *Lucretia Borgia* (Abel Gance, 1935) in which the great lady of the French cinema, Edwige Feuillere, played her first commercial role, contains feasts that inevitably end with tumbling of the feminine dinner partners, by the separation of their thighs — and by the artful abandon of the viewer to his own appetite. Remaking it in color and with Martine Carol, Christian Jacques took care not to succumb to these picturesque temptations. Jacques Feyder in *Carnival in Flanders* (1935) tells of the arrival of the Spanish (in the seventeenth century) at a Flemish village, and depicts the imaginary fears of the inhabitants. According to them, the first act of these tough troopers will be to charge through the city, inventorying the women in order to subject them to the ultimate violation. These feasts or these sackings have in common the fault of wanting to disguise the brutality in this aggressiveness. Pranksters, strapping fellows, bold hussies, all abandon themselves too quickly in the worst Rabelaisian activity. The Japanese are a more scrupulous people. At the Gate of Hell brigands have raped a woman and killed her husband. *Rashamon* (Kurasawa, 1950) will follow Pirandello's technique and therefore vainly attempt to discover what really happened by scrutinizing the evidence. But at least the repetitions permits us to see Machiko Kyo going through variations on the theme of violation in a dreamlike atmosphere that, aided by the great talent of the best Japanese director, sharply evokes the episode of the Heart of Iron in *Justine*. Finally, the history of the American West offers the rapes of Marlene Dietrich in *Rancho Notorious* (Fritz Lang, 1952) and of Maria Schell *Hangman's Hill* (Delmer Davis, 1958); and political history, the history of racism supplies the rape of Mae Marsh by the Negro, Gus (Walter Long) in *Birth of a Nation* (Griffith, 1915).

History, from which ordinary politics stem, as everyone knows, by other methods, should be closely linked to war. Military rape sometimes takes the appearance of gaiety. The marine, according to his most proficient painter, Raoul Walsh, thinks only of sexual joking, from gross banter to the most subtle limerick, and keeps his eye obstinately fixed, not on the blue line of the Pacific as one commonly believes, but on the silhouettes (dreamed and streamlined) of seductresses, prostitutes, Wacs, girl friends, nurses, natives and other captives of his direct and conquering virility, (*Battle Cry,* 1954; *The Naked and the Dead,* 1950). But when the locale changes, things become more serious. Invading the islands of the Pacific, Japs hurl themselves at the whites who can not escape in time, *The Purple Heart* (Lewis Milestone, 1944),

The Odyessy of Dr. Wassel (Cecil B. DeMille, 1944). The
Nazis, occupying Europe, exercised the right of the Lord of
War over the Italians, as in the recent *Ultimatum alla Vita*
(Ranato Polselli, 1962).

Diametrically opposite, at least in principle, although the
story of Sadie Thompson leaves a lingering doubt, is the religious rape. It is the violent fruit, sometimes murderous, of
thou-shalt-nots and other prohibitions. We will wait a long
time before a producer offers, and even longer until a censor
allows, the creation of *"The Abominable Story of the Vicar
of Uruffe,"* or various minor scandals, even more skillfully
stifled. It is necessary to be content with metaphysical-symbolic
parables which cannot expose to full light the preoccupations
labelled shameful, and therefore allowed to grow into obses-
sions. Rape will not be shown as the savage and blind release
of absurdly restrained tendencies, but as an outrage pagan in
origin, and as an irreligious assault on sacrosanct virginity.
In the Middle Ages all virgins wandering in the woods had to
be violently deflowered and then strangled by the travelers
they encountered. *The Virgin Spring* (Ingmar Bergmann,
1960) found a gold mine of publicity by priding itself on
presenting the most detailed rape in the history of the movies.
God, need it be said, sanctifies the victim: a stream, possibly
symbolic, spurting forth and flowing, is the evidence of his
grace, since it is without humor. Even more saintly is the
maiden who determines to kill herself before the satyr can
attain his goal. Maria Goretti will be canonized for having,
at the price of her life, refused a very earthy love offered by
a farm boy of such profound stupidity that this results in
making him furiously mad. *Ciello Sulla Palude* (Augusto
Genina, known elsewhere for his career as a fascist filmmaker)
is worth considering for a moment. The confused morality of
the film is revealed by a talent that bizarrely transforms that

which it wishes to denounce. In it, desire is painted with a touch of the oppressive, an attraction towards the symbolic— oh that forked tree!—and to sum it up, a natural penchant for perversity which would, by its persistence, cause some doubt about the purity of the author's intentions, *The Girl of the Swamp* (1949).

It is first in the Protestant church, Baptist if memory serve, that we find a lucid denunciation of this ambiguity. Maugham's novel "Rain" (where Sadie, the whore, lands on a Pacific island for a soldier's pleasure but winds up violated by the minister, who, amorous and paralyzed by fear of the flesh, finds no other way of satisfying his desire) has had three versions. In the first Gloria Swanson was directed by the inevitable Walsh (1928); in the second, Joan Crawford by Milestone (1932); and Rita Hayworth by Bernhart, in the third (1954). Finally, there is the Sabbat where conscious, at last, the antiChristian revolt takes on the very look of the sexual revolt. In comparison with the shabby orgies of Guil- laume Radot (*Guillemette Babin,* 1947), the clinical demon- stration, the admirable, full-blown enrichment by Benjamin Christiansen must be vastly preferred: *Witchcraft Through the Ages* (Haxan) in 1920, where the relation between nightmare and hysteria is clearly revealed.

Rape is considered a crime punished by law; it forms a completely natural sector of this troubled universe whose artificial frontiers are drawn with little regard to the natural boundaries of Society. Thus, the world of the prohibition bootleggers in the United States provided one of the most famous literary examples of rape. Temple Drake, heroine of Faulkner's "Sanctuary" is raped by the vagrant Popeye. As he is far from having the vigor of his homonymous namesake (the cartoon hero drawn by Segar), he is fundamentally im- potent and has to use an ear of corn to complete the job.

It is understood that in the two adaptations of the Nobel prizewinner (*The Story of Temple Drake*) 1933, with Miriam Hopkins as Temple and Jack La Rue as Popeye; and *Sanctuary,* Tony Richardson, 1960, with Lee Remick as Temple and Yves Montand as Popeye, this episode though important (not to say essential) to the story is carefully passed over. Without it, the narrative loses all truthfulness, all impact. This, in fact, did happen to these two films. By contrast, the rape of the idiot Marietta (Melvina Polo) by the noble and martial Count Serge Karamzin (Eric von Stroheim) had been in *Foolish Wives* (Stroheim, 1921) evoked with a profusion of detail — consistent with the film's readiness to construct an elaborate Monte Carlo in California. In these cases, the victim is always given a vague additional disgrace, meant to make her more pitiable to compassionate hearts; but also to make the brutality which befalls her more natural, to make her path (why not say it) easier for her. If, therefore, the destiny of *Johnny Belinda* (Henry Negulesco, 1948) (who, deaf and dumb, couldn't even cry out, if only for form's sake when she saw her virtue in danger) provokes horror, it also arouses a certain repulsion for Jane Wyman before her misfortune. Woman, thus dominated, humiliated, ravished for the particular pleasure of the viewer, serves in another sense as the cause of misogyny, as puritans or Catholics very clearly perceive.

Finally, let us rapidly go on to another social form of rape. The modern incarnation of the right of the conqueror, the factor in society that reveals itself by its ready sexual submission, when confronted by force. Elsa Martinelli's rape, perpetrated in front of a crowd that was almost unaware of it and, about which the K of *Proces* (Orson Welles, 1962) becomes indignant, is certainly an extreme symbol of the affirmation of power, in this case martial power. But Klinckart

(Paul Meyer) tells a very real anecdote. In the brickfields of the Anvers region in Flanders, by tradition and training the girl workers, braving the derisive laughter of their fellow-workers who sully their image, are compelled to make love with the boss to keep from losing their jobs. To those whom this surprises or who react with dread, we offer the myth of the amorous secretary, the humble and charming young lady who marries the rich director, a myth naively exploited, often not without skill, *I Married My Boss* (Gregory La Cava, 1934), or very adroitly exposed as by the adorable cynic, Louis Brooks, *Love Them or Leave Them* (1928).

BRIDE OF GORILLA AND ROBOT

The entire tradition of animalism conceived, not as substitute but as intensification, witnesses that masochism may, like aggressiveness, take extreme forms as in rape. Amateurs and historians can refer to Jean Boullet's "Beauty and the Beast." They will find there rich material to feed the course of their precious studies. We will limit ourselves here, to strictly cinematographic aspects.

The anomalous being, the monster who carries off the heroine, preferably clad in a long white robe, is a familiar and favorite character of movie fans. His proto-and-archetype is the sleepwalker of the *Cabinet of Dr. Caligari*.

To each master his due: the king of the jungle, the gigantic anthropoid gorilla, alone holds sway in this precious domain, appreciated by the few elect, secretly envied by their companions. "I don't know what he sees in her," comments the matronly white resident contemptuously, jealously watching the ape carrying a young woman to his lair. The gambols of Tarzan's various heroines (apeman himself, to be sure, but in this too much the man to carry on with Cheeta, the chim-

panzee) remain simple, inoffensive amusements compared
to the more robust pleasures tasted by the heroine of *Nabonga*
(Sam Neufeld). "A young girl raised in the jungle by a giant
gorilla was found several years later living intimately with her
hairy companion. One of the most curious scenes of this film
shows us a veritable duel between two apes, fighting for the
charms of pretty Julie London." The multiple examples of
these loves in the trees are known in France only by tradition.
We weren't able to see either the *Bride of the Gorilla,* by
the specialist in fantasy, Curt Siodmak, or *Lovelife of a Gorilla,* heralded by an attractive publicity poster. Unfortunately,
we know how little credence as to the promised emotional experience — I mean by that anything having to do with the
actual contents of the film — we place in the cliches the
movie distributors spread in the press to catch naive readers.

Man and the dream mix happily. Charles Laughton in the
Island of Dr. Moreau (Erle C. Kenton), a film extraordinarily
rich in half-man, half-beast creatures, sacrifices his panther
wife, Kathleen Burke, for reasons that are not purely scientific. The different adaptations of Poe's *Murders in the Rue
Morgue* (Robert Florey, 1931; Roy del Ruth, 1955), make
the young heroine borne by the murderous and monstrous ape
a respectable role, whereas Eric von Stroheim's *Mad Doctor*
surrenders Hildegarde Neff, the beautiful android, to an equally
lustful simian. Finally, at the peak of the cult of giantism one
must place the famous scene from *King Kong* (Schoedsack
and Cooper 1933) where the cyclopean gorilla, having come
from a lost world, meticulously peels Fay Wray's clothing;
and also *Mighty Joe Young* (1949, Schoedsack) which marks
the paradoxical but charming invention of courtly love by
the titans.

Half-man half-beast — in combining the potentialities of
the first with all the ravishing and brutal power of the second,

one must discuss the werewolf, the man who transforms himself into a hairy monster, on the nights of the full moon;
thanks to the make-up man, Jack Pierce, to terrorize the
adorable girls in nightclothes. Let us cite the *Wolf Man*
(George Wagner, 1948), who is most faithfully dedicated to
the legend, and the *Curse of the Werewolf* (Terence Fisher,
1951), where one waits much too long to see the beautiful
Yvonne Roman in the clutches of a man-animal, who is
perhaps a touch too wavy-haired.

Emerging from a swamp in the Amazons, amphibian man
has, so they say, erotic attractions which are altogether new,
according to specialists of both sexes whom we haven't any
reason to doubt. Jack Arnold produced, with his customary
talent, the first two films of the series: *The Creature of the
Black Lagoon,* 1954 and the *Revenge of the Creature,* 1955.
From the point of view that interests us here, the originality
is doublebarreled. The monster is presented as a jealous
madman; and the beauty is unfailingly clothed in a bathing
costume. Perhaps one should nevertheless prefer the third
panel in the series, produced by John Sherwood, the *Creature
Walks Among Us,* 1957, where the Creature, less physically
a monster, does not content himself with fury but very hu-
manly recognizes the sadness of unrequited passion. Let us
consider the molemen, *The Mole People* (Virgil Vogel), and
the hideous mutants who inhabit the atomized earth of 2950;
and let us deplore the regrettable misuse by which Jean Cocteau converted, as was his wont, a myth that is not without
charm. *Beauty and the Beast,* 1946 (where playing opposite
to the insipid Josette Day, Jean Marais is transformed into an
adorable tomcat) converted the story of Madame LePrince of
Beaumont into a matter of windy rooms, and the monster into
a pussycat Drouant.

The ugly man, ugliness itself, is in fact a plausible substitute for animality. Without doubt, this is based on the instinctive connection, incorrectly esablished, between the beauty of a man and a degree of femininization. The interpretors of Dr. Jekyll, are, as Mr. Hyde, doubly ugly, mean, and twice as bestial as the man. They force unhappy but fascinating prostitutes to submit to the worst brutalities; whether it is the best of them all, John Barrymore (Robertson, 1920) or Frederic March (Rouben Manoulian, 1932) or Spencer Tracy (Victor Fleming, 1941). In the last manifestation of Stevenson's novel, the evil *Will of Dr. Cordelier* (Jean Renoir, 1960), the police, in penetrating Jean Louis Barrault's lair regard with horror (which can only represent the high morality, as well as the naivete, of the producer), the collection of riding crops and whips decorating the sinister man's room.

Eric, the hero of *Phantom of the Opera,* was so disfigured that his face resembled a death's head. One must dismiss as negligible the interpretations by Claude Raines, in Arthur Lubin's version and Herbert Lom in Terence Fisher's (1961) and come to Lon Chaney's which outclasses, once and for all, its followers (including that dominated by Rupert Julian) and thus explains these others. Ravished, the heroine was led along mysterious corridors, then along a subterranean lake, obscured by fog, and hemmed in by vaults that introduced a thundering romanticism into a myth that demanded something better, since Hugo himself had indicated precisely all the coordinates of the myth in his Quasimodo of Notre Dame of Paris. Quasimodo was admirably incarnated by Charles Laughton, under the direction of William Dieterle, 1939, and, let us say less well, by Anthony Mann under the glossy shepherd's crook of Jean Delanoy, 1960. Monsters could make love among themselves, but these revels, as fascinating as their horrors are, do not fall within the already too broad bounds of our subject, cinematographic sadism (*Freaks,* Tod Browning, 1932; Fraser, *Love Among the Monsters*).

If zombies, as mechanized slaves from beyond the grave, cannot awaken in themselves spark or desire, it is otherwise for mummies. From the *Mummy* (Karl Freund, 1932) to the *Curse of the Pharoahs* (Terence Fisher) from Boris Karloff to Christopher Lee, and from Zita Johann to the marvelous Yvonne Furneaux, the Yvonne of the British cinema, the general schema does not change. The mummy is an Egyptian priest, magically brought back to life, who in modern times searches for and finally finds the reincarnation of his former love. He takes her away, as he should; but, actually, in vain. *The Mummy's Ghost,* Reginald Le Borg, merits specific notice. The action takes place on an American college campus, the heroine, a young Egyptian student, courts a young American who is quite obtuse. The Mummy passes several times during the night. Each time, as if warned by a presentiment, the girl goes to meet him, and as soon as she sees him, faints. Each time — without ever explaining the phenomenon in the dialogue — a lock of her hair whitens. At the end, when the mummy goes off with his beloved, he carries in his arms a marvellous creature whose hair is as white as molten silver. Pursued, the couple flees through a series of beautiful sets and when he is finally engulfed in a swamp under the eye of the helpless young American, the closeup reveals the impossible and horrible reality: the girl has become a mummy in her turn.

The humanoid monsters created from fragments of cadavers by Dr. Frankenstein have less success among beautiful mortals, but not for want of trying — menacing or carrying off, as chance permits, the heroine. In *Frankenstein* (James Whale, 1931), Boris Karloff, in a scene that has remained famous, threatens Mae Clark dressed (no detail could be more piquant) in a bridal gown, before he goes on, in all purity of course, to play with a little girl; these scenes are incidentally among the most beautiful of a very rich film. These last incarnations, by this I mean the English ones, the *Curse of Frankenstein* (Terence Fisher, 1957), showed more subtlety in the human dehumanization, but greater calm at the level of appetite.

In fact, it was time that the robot of flesh yield place as a ravisher to the robot of metal. The man from outer space, Klatou, in the *Day the Earth Stood Still* (Robert Wise, 1951) has an electronic servant that terrifies Patricia Neal before carrying her helplessly off, in the flying saucer which brought it. The same is true in *Earth vs. Flying Saucers.* Similarly, in *Forbidden Planet* (Fred McLeod Wilcox, 1957) where Robby is a faithful servant, endowed with humor, and surely with robust special talents, if one accepts the meaningful way he carries Anne Francis in his arms. In any event, their metallic purity is, modern for modern, preferable to the vile creatures of space, mutants of the planet Metalluna, with visible brains and with lobster arms, whose designs on the heroine are as problematic as unacknowledgable; or those even more ignoble creatures, a kind of enormous ape-spider with eyes like headlights and fingers featuring suction cups, who bound out of flying saucers in *War of the Worlds,* not to mention the monster animated by Jack Arnold *They Came from Outer Space,* 1950, whose appearance — originally in 3-D, made in France — petrifies a young scientist with puzzled horror.

Whatever the menace, its sexual purpose cannot be doubted; one must, in any event, note the total absence of wooing. What seduces in regard to the gorilla, the monster, or the robot is, above all, its simple violence, enhanced by fetishism. It remained for another sort of monster, the vampire, to develop prestige, moral even if morbid, in its seductions.

THE SLAP

By its very spontaneity — because it occurs without thinking, by reflex — the slap is at the zero degree of conscious
violence. That it is not planned, makes it the method of elemental brutality. But at the same time, the intention to avoid
too great physical damage — the open hand replaces the
closed fist — reinforces its moral violence. Readers of the
"Cid" know that between men the slap is a mortal insult that
must be washed out with blood. Heterosexually, it is preeminently the method and the symbol of domination.

In the movies, its occurrence marks a climax in an amorous
intrigue. At the highest point of irritation, Edouard Gelin slaps
Caroline-Anne Vernon, and their affair is changed by it.
(*Edouard and Caroline*, Jacques Becker). The same Gelin
(*Appointment in July* also by Becker) surprises the girl he
loves, Nicol Coursel, semi-nude, in another man's room. The
smack he gives her makes her understand just how great his
outrage is. A reconciliation is not far off, one surmises. Nor
is repentance. Similarly, Trintignant finding Brigitte Bardot,
his wife, about to expose herself while dancing before an
appreciative audience, in an hysterical cha-cha-cha, slaps her
magnificently before taking her home (*And God Created
Woman*, Roger Vadim, 1956). Just as moralizing is the slap
George Sanders gives Anne Baxter in *All About Eve* (Joseph
Mankiewicz, 1957).

As well as being a simple and efficacious manner of putting
fiancees, wives and mistresses on the right path, the slap is the
easiest way for the male to affirm his power. Although a tired
hero, Montand summons up the strength to slap Maria Felis
hard enough to reestablish the natural hierarchy (*The Tired
Heroes*, Yves Ciampi, 1955). Rosanna Podesta, by dint of her
maddening arousal of her companion's concupiscence with

teasing gossamer garb created by Alex Philip, ends by having herself soundly cuffed (*La Red,* Emilio Fernandez, 1953). In order to establish his role as chief Nazi sadist Robert Rossein, directed by Roger Vadim, finds no better way than to slap Annie Girardot until she falls.

Anger by the way, need not be involved. Jean Paul Belmondo, in *Le Doulos,* questions Monique Hennessy, his friend's mistress, with perfect calm, and with a politeness that, though scarcely elaborate, is quite sincere. The blows, as violent as could be wished, are all the more efficacious, because nothing telegraphs them, not the slightest raising of the voice. Let us make it clear all the same, to obviate all equivocation, that this rather ignoble scene has absolutely nothing Baudelairean about it (Jean-Pierre Melville, 1963).

At a higher level, the slap is a proof of love, a form that is a little more sophisticated, a little more brutal than the caress, to which it adds not a touch of irritation. But here it has only a limited range. Richard Widmark in *Pick Up on South Street* (1953), stops slapping Anne Francis only to cover her with kisses. Claude Mann, in the *Bay of Angels,* to the spectators' great satisfaction, gets around to slapping Jean Moreau, but this is just to manage a better fall on the nearest sofa with her (Jacques Demy, 1962). More rarely, this little game becomes homosexual, Jack Palance in *Panic in the Streets,* Elia Kazan (1950), dances around a dying person that he's trying to make talk, a strange ballet in which he mixes smacks, blows, caresses and passionate declarations. In *Hiroshima, Mon Amour* (Alain Resnais, 1959), as well as in *The Angel of Death* (Luis Bumuel, 1962), and further, in *Blood on the Sun* (Frank Lloyd, 1939), apologies and declarations of love follow the slaps. But we are here concerned with the lower stage — apology after the abrupt release of exasperation; rather than discussing the prolongation, that, incidentally, characterized the Golden Age. Violence in itself does not seem to have had an effect on Emmanuelle Riva, Sylvia Pinal, or Sylvia Sidney.

After these diverse approximations one must face up to what is now the archetype in the cinema, the passionate slap. This involves the slap that Glenn Ford deals to Rita Hayworth, in an enduring challenge to public attitudes, by the authors of the wild *Gilda* (1945). The publicity and the success of the film were entirely set, happily in part by mistake, around the worshiping heroine, huddled at the feet of the dominant male who has just slapped her. This triumph amazed Columbia so much that they hurried to reunite the same partners with the sole purpose of repeating the scene where the man slaps the woman. This was how *Affair of Trinidad* was born (Vincent Sherman, 1946), and *The Loves of Carmen* (Charles Vidor, 1947, who strangely, lost inspiration). Thus, the slap knew its highest point of glory in its decadence. A sense of the scabrous so elaborated, even if this scabrousness, utilized only fairly elementary means, leads us much further, and certainly deeper, than the exchange of slaps, in the French style, by which outraged virtues defend themselves, and thanks to which over-excited nerves find release, exchanges which strew the ineffable *Du Mouron pour les petits Oiseaux* (Marcel Carne, 1962).

SPANKING

For the historian of customs as for the writer of memoirs of sensitivity, the development of a taste for spanking, in letters and art in the 20th century, offers a subject of study as fresh as it would be absorbing. Among the forbidden books (as well as those that manage to pass through the vigilant censorship of the mails because they are not in the strict sense of the word pornographic), I would be willing to bet that at least a thousand novels — reckoning only those in French, although everything leads us to believe there is an equally rich production in English and German — make spanking their essential spring, if not their exclusive subject.

It would be vain to believe this is a spontaneous blossoming. The foreshadowings of this modern flowering are as numerous as they are ancient. But one must admit that since the end of the 19th century one is in the presence of a rise so brutal that in our times the spanking has become the privileged form of what may be called minor sadism, a harmonious mixture of pain, slight in itself, and a ceremony which by making ridiculous, emphasizes its humiliating character, followed by the double arousal, active and passive.

It may be conceded that the movies could not neglect this rich vein.

The spanking is in the first place, and this is an added charm, a pedagogical punishment. Without doubt, the trailblazer's prize must be given to the street sprinkler who was mystified by the child's sprinkling him in *The Sprinkler Sprinkled* (1895, Louis Luniere). That child's bruised behind is the precursor of these, cited at random: Jack Pickford, Jackie Coogan, and Tommy Kelly in their various versions of *Tom Sawyer* (William Desmond, 1917, John Cromwell, 1930; then Norman Taurog, in color 1937), Freddy Bartholomew (*David Copperfield,* George Cukor, 1935) and the unlucky heroes of *The War of the Buttons* (Yves Robert, 1962). *Hellfire Club* (Robert S. Baker and Monty Berman, 1960) *Miss Doctor* (G. W. Pabst, 1937), and some I have intentionally overlooked. In these punishments, however, the erotic value is limited, if not totally missing. They are offered for what they are, painful punishments, and can even rise to a brutal cruelty which, a priori, excludes all sexual overtones as in *The Child-*

hood of Gorki (Mark Donskoy, 1938). The heroine of *Hungry Hill* (Brian Desmond Hurst, 1955), on the contrary, wants to protect Anthony Wager and diverts the wrath of his grandfather who, brush in hand, sternly awaits the little boy. The *Invisible Boy* (Herman Hoffman) who although completely invisible, has still not escaped reproof, by his father (based on dead reckoning) is protected from the ultimate punishment by Robby the Robot, adherent of a pedagogy less attached to the old-fashioned way.

A hint of sophistication, though very rarely linked to nudity, is regularly found in Mack Sennett comedies, for example. Having undertaken to spank several little boys and girls for playing tricks on him, Chester Conklin makes them line up, in a file, on their knees, so that he may more easily give them each a few smacks. To make sure the blows register better, he raises the skirts of the girls, stopping modestly and lowering them abruptly when the guilty party happens not to be wearing drawers. This complexity, here in its embryonic state, soon becomes more specific. At the end of their terrifying nocturnal flight, the young heroes of *Night of the Hunter* find refuge in the home of an old lady, sister of the nursery rhyme heroine who housed many children in a shoe, archetype of the mother-hen, the protectress. An early manifestation of this mothering involves the good woman taking under her arm and spanking, naked as a pin, the little boy who doesn't want to wash. One can find reassurance in Charles Laughton. Spanking is utterly alien to an innocence to which it would seem to be a return.

In the literary classics, at least, the French punishment of children seems not to have found a brilliant cinematic career. *The Misfortunes of Sophie,* directed by Jacqueline Audry in 1946, did not even obscurely hint that the governess Marguerite Moreno might let herself go at the seat of her pupil,

Madeleine Rousset, who was bizarrely raised to the rank of a revolutionary heroine in 1830. The greatest mystery hovers over the incompleted *Model Little Girls* by Eric Rohmer as well as over the secret *A Good Little Devil* by Claude de Givray. This equivocal ancestor of the fearful Jojo had been well-enacted, rich with ambiguity, by Mary Pickford; not having seen the film, I can not discuss in detail the episodes of interest here. Very recently, in a television broadcast by Claude Santelli, a Scotsman played by Joel Flatteau, receives a few whacks with a switch — modestly on his breeches' bottom.

In the United States, the famous Katzenjammer Kids, by Rudolph Dirks, were the heroes of animated cartoons directed by Robert Allen, and especially by William Hannah. Of the series *Captain and the Kids* I have seen only the *Captain's Christmas,* rigorously devoid of corporal punishments. The presence of one of the future fathers of Tom and Jerry permits one to suppose nevertheless, that in the others ah! . . . Also, Jimmy Hatlo's heroine, *Little Iodine* reached the screen where, under the direction of Reginald Le Borg, in 1946, she was played by Jo Ann Marlowe. In the comic strip she was regularly spanked by her father Mr. Tremblechin (Howard Cavanaugh), in the course of an incessant battle, a war in which the unfortunate girl has habitually suffered defeat in the end.

This kind of relation between father and daughter leads us, finally, to the most interesting point in the discussion.

These are matters that do not change, except to match the taste of the times, and as the age of the feminine victims becomes more important. What used to be the punishment of children, thorny bushes along the green-bordered paths of Paradise, becomes more than a stinging pain — an insupportable humiliation. Recall the last letter of Zachi, one of his favorites, to Usbek: "Oh Heavens! a barbarian insulted me by the very way in which he punished me! He inflicted a chastisement on me which began by frightening my modesty, this chastisement which actually brings back childhood" (Persian Letters" CLVII). Times have changed, the timid, emotional excitement replaces outraged self-respect; Montesquieu's heroine would recognize her cinematic sister with great difficulty, and find it even harder to locate a compassionate viewer, since frank, or embarrassed, laughter is the ineluctable reaction of the public to this sort of thing. Revolt is lightly sketched, in passing, in *Adam's Rib*, (George Cukor, 1949). Katherine Hepburn cannot stand the least masculine superiority, being herself dominating. She is spread out on a massage table, and to finish the session her husband, Spencer Tracy, gives her one of those jovial and resounding smacks, a habit he had certainly acquired by watching Ford and Walsh's films. She bristles and makes a scene, accusing him of concealing ulterior motives of domination behind this joke. "You hit me," she reproves him with violence, "as if you thought you had the right!" Perhaps there was the same sort of frankness when the charming Maggie MacNamara in *The Moon is Blue* (Otto Preminger, 1953) looks with distrust at David Niven, poised to flee when she learns that he had spanked his wife with, (horrible detail) a pie-plate.

But these threats are even less effective on grown-up Shirley Temple; and the apprehension that swells her attractive bobby-soxer chest, when her uncle threatens to treat her like a bad little child (*The Bachelor and the Bobby Soxer*, Irving Reis), succeeds only with great difficulty in appearing merely timid. Similarly, when Burt Lancaster assures Virginia Mayo that should the occasion arise he would not hesitate "to spank her like a girl at home" the young woman doesn't seem particularly offended (*The Flame and the Arrow*, Jacques Tourneur,

1950). Let us discuss, finally, the gap between the threat and the promise. In *Bluebeard* (Christian Jacque, 1950), Cecile Aubry makes a lovely game of whimpering while rubbing her seat after we have seen her pursued by peasants; her attitude and her face permit a feeling appreciably different from simple pain to become apparent. The morality of these attitudes is given in a charming dialogue between two female students, an unexpected bonus, in the Willy Rozier movie *Manina the Girl Without a Veil,* better known for having given Brigitte Bardot (after the *Trouble of Normandy*) her second role (let it be clear that she was neither of the two speakers). "How can you," says the first, "stay with a guy who dishes out slaps," and the second offers this excuse, as obvious as it is natural; "Oh, but they're not always on the cheeks!" This gratification finds a certain echo in the audience. One need only witness that, when the heroine of whatever film finds herself spanked, the spectators laugh with embarrassment but really with appreciation, to be convinced of its unquestionable allure.

The victims are usually rather young girls, really child-women and, correspondingly, the torturers are middle-aged men. Jean Marais, in maturity, will always be the spanker found by the little darling. In the *Iron Mask* (Henri Decoin, 1962) he pursues her, takes her in his arms, lifts her skirts and spanks the bottom of a white panty — perhaps a little anachronistic, but its presence adds piquancy to the scene. Other times, other places, same customs: Clark Gable in the primitive America of the pre-Western seats himself on a tree stump, near a raging stream, puts his young Indian wife Maria Elena Marques over his knees and spanks her while a sardonic medicine man shakes a sort of rattle to punctuate the blows. (*Across the Wide Missouri,* William Wellman, 1951). Seated on the modern benches of Munich's Great Wheel, Carlos Thompson chastises the featherbrained Romy

Schneider in *Eve, the Diaries of a Young Girl* (Die Halbzarte) by Rolf Thiele; the parents of the wench when acquainted with the situation can only approve this severity. The same Shirley Temple who graduated unscathed from a long line of childish melodramas attains, at adolesence, the opportunity not only to be threatened, but actually to be smacked effectively with a brush (*Honeymoon,* 1947) by the poor man whose too youthful wife she is. It is hardly necessary to specify the allusions to the sweet and strong paternal power these adolescents are going to look for; the psychoanalysis would be easy. Douglas Sirk who showed us Rock Hudson in the act of spanking Barbara Rush in *Captain Lightfoot* (1955), a year earlier showed us (*Taza, Son of Cochise*) a father threatening his daughter with the same punishment. In the following year he must have perfected his theory of the Electra Complex and he depicts for us, at the denouement of *Written on the Wind,* Dorothy Malone, daughter of a rich Texas oilman, who nostalgically caresses a miniature derrick, an ambiguous but remarkably lucid symbol of the power of her dead and passionately mourned father. The spanking administered to her grown daughter by Sophia Loren in *Two Women* appears completely incongruous in such context. It is true that elsewhere it would be difficult to discern in Vittorio de Sica's uniformly commonplace mind the least pretension to an erotic sophistication.

Vastly remote from psychoanalytic dramas, the spanking is an opportunity for "French style" spectacles of a friendly sexuality, akin to the exhibition of underwear backsides in the French can-can and always contrived with the tone of a candid lark. It is one of the spices of Fernandel movies such as *Adrien* directed in 1943 by the comedian himself, or another (the title of which I have forgotten) in which the punishment has the originality of being administreed by a collier, thus leaving black handprints on the victim's skirt. Derived from Courtelin, the spanking episode of the play "Peace At Home" is effectively shown in Berthomieu's film *Family Scenes* (Scenes de Menage) where Francois Perrier chastises Marie Daems; it is at an even lower stage that Jean de Letraz' *The Spanking* was brought to the screen in 1937 by Pierre Caron. If there is merit in the debatable pleasure of seeing Ed Constantine perform base acts (*Les Femmes s' en Balancent,* Borderie) on the person of Nadia Gray, then there will also be value in the more subtle joy of seeing Elke Sommer punished by her timorous lover, suddenly freed of his illusions, under the enraptured and admiring eyes of Darry Cowl (*Les Bricoleurs; The Jacks of All Trades;* Jean Girault, 1962).

Certain French actresses appear to be dedicated from the start of their careers to this type of bruise. It is true that some were specialists in the role of the insupportable wife, and this explains it: the multiple chastisements which Sophie Desmarets, or even Dany Robin received, first at the hands of Georges Marshall, then from O. W. Fisher. One of these frankly admitted the taste she had, in actuality, for this type of situation. Suzy Delair went as far as having a photo of herself published (in which she appeared in an inviting position under the arm of an obliging reporter) on the front page of France-Dimanche.

American comedy, as always, had to purify and stylize this situation. At first, Lubitsch was the gourmet, and Harold Lloyd, that idealization of the American man, took pleasure in bringing back in *The World of Harold Lloyd* (1961) a shot of an old film where he is seen, hairbrush in hand, threatening the seat of a lady, flat on her stomach across his knees. The most famous couples often give themselves up to this pastime. William Powell spanked Myrna Loy in *After the Thin Man* (Woody S. Van Dyck, 1936). Frederic March spanked Carole Lombard in *Nothing Sacred* (William Wellman, 1937). The war passed. John Carroll spanked Susan Hayward in *My Foolish Heart* (Mark Robeson, 1949). Nor are these the only examples.

One should not believe that the United States denied itself the embellishments that old and sophisticated Europe was permitted. *So This is New York* (Richard Fleischer, 1948) although not released in France, was nonetheless the object of ingenious publicity. Photographs of the film were spread around, in which the hero was seen spanking a charming soubrette, who at the end of the film would become his wife, but who at the moment displayed a very wicked little black panty. In 1963, the English followed this good example and published in "Cinemonde" trailer photos of *The Iron Maiden* where Michael Craig spanks Anne Helm, and of *The Saint,* after Leslie Charteris, where Roger Moore spanks Anica Rogers.

Because it has sure-fire comic elements, the spanking comes to serve as an interlude in the drama. In *The Roots of the Sky* Errol Flynn, under the direction of John Huston, can relax his nerves, and for a moment relieve the spectators' tension, by spanking a too-enthusiastic elephant huntress. Conversely, its utterly absurd intrusion in the already absurd *Animal Crackers* by Victor Heermann (1930) provokes feelings of uneasiness. In the course of a very select ball, a dancer suddenly stops, grabs his partner and spanks her — for absolutely no reason. That this is a little sister of the famous tumbril scene in *The Golden Age,* will be recognized.

Even the Western is not exempt. *Frontier Gal* (Charles Lamont, 1945) has a particularly exemplary outcome. Halfway in the film, Rod Cameron spanks his little girl, with whom he has just decided to live. She, completely happy although in tears, thanks her father for finally treating her "like other little girls". And when at the end, it is Yvonne de Carlo's turn to be spread across Cameron's thighs and get a spanking, the little girl, drawing heavily on her personal experience, announces the lesson of the situation: "If he beats you, it's because he loves you." A dull young woman, until then the hero's fiancee, horrified, must yield her place to the saloon singer, since she is incapable of accepting, like her, the moral level of the old West — rude in appearance but subtle at the bottom.

Literature has an equivalent of this business. In *Kiss Me Kate* (George Sidney), Howard Keel, the hero of the musical, uses a performance of "The Taming of the Shrew" as a pretext for really spanking Virginia Grey on stage, and thus provoking a general scandal. The film was, in the original but not when shown in France, so designed as to add to the scene a quality of perfection. In the many versions of Zola's "L'Assommoir" homage is paid to the famous spanking in the washhouse. In the last version *Gervaise* by Rene Clement, Suzy Delair is seen stretched out on the ground with Maria Schell sitting astride her, facing backwards. Maria raises Suzy's skirts, and opens the flap of her drawers (a rare boldness which the connoisesseur appreciates although the rear end of the actress is covered) and jolts to the blows of the paddle on the buttocks of her victim (1956).

As we see, the spanking often provided the happy days of the commercial cinema; but it is necessary to add that it equally nourished the equivalent cinema of the nickelodeons of the boulevards, before they were converted to strip-teases as varigated as they were monotonous.

Ado Kyrou ("Love-Eroticism and the Movies") cites one of these films: "A student of six (usually played by a girl twice that age) badly recites her fables from La Fontaine. Her overworked instructress, lifts the child's skirts and beats her ferociously with a strap; then she ties her to a tree and, for no reason, tears off her dress" (p. 332). I myself know of two others. In the first, the mother and daughter are going on a picnic, the daughter breaks the plates. The mother corners her, puts her across her knees, and begins to spank her, having lifted up her dress. As the "child" struggles, the mother lowers her drawers to smack her with greater ease. Then she lets her go. The daughter, drawers about her knees, gets up and continues carrying the plates, and breaks others. The mother grabs her again, and spanks her once more; and so forth through several repetitions. In the second, a haughty and very elegant young woman gets into her beautiful car and drives away. On the road she is stopped by a hitch-hiker, a little fellow, skinny and bearded, whom she insults. The man becomes enraged, opens the door, pulls the girl from her seat, turns her on her stomach on the fender, lifts her dress and profits from the fact that she is not wearing underpants to spank her nakedness. A systematic investigation, very difficult today, would certainly provide an ample harvest of these short films with pleasantly absurd scenarios.

One might possibly be surprised that the victims of these chastisings are exclusively female, but it should be recognized that the reverse situation would really be too ridiculous. In "General History of the Movies" by Georges Sadoul (vol. III, part 1) one can see Andre Deed, disguised as a little boy, spread flat on his stomach across the knees of a robust maid-servant whose punitive intentions are evident. But there it is a matter of burlesque, and not the best (by Cretinelli from Italy, around 1908). It is therefore better to conclude by returning to the question of the moment, admiring, in *The Merry Widow* (Werner Jacobs, 1963), the Viennese spanking of Genevieve Cluny by Peter Alexander, under the envious glances of politely undressed girls. The Austrian movies do have the advantage of pretty girls and color.

The Whip

"If you whip, you are cruel; in a libertine, thrashing is only the outburst of his ferocity: it is in order to give him an outlet that he comes to it. He would do something else if he dared." These aphorisms of Juliette admirably define the privileged place of whipping in sadism. The spanking has great, but different merits and is ineffective, in any case, in exciting the pleasure of cruel libertines. Whipping applies to the whole body, with the aid of various instruments which have the common function of wounding, while smacks only serve to redden. In addition whipping is more obviously dishonoring. While the spanking still has some of the characteristics of a game, and recalls the obscure hurts of childhood, the pain of the whip is that which is applied to slaves, prisoners, and inferiors. For the one that orders it, or the one that carries it out, it is the sign of absolute, essential power; and for the victim, the harrowing proof of his actual inferiority, and his eventual submission. The pleasure of the participants is not as obvious as in the preceding chapter, but it is no less likely; and is all the more violent.

If whipping does not have, as does spanking, an originally pedagogical purpose, it falls just as hard upon children. But here lie greater nostalgias, deeper complexes. Oedipus, Electra and Orestes yield their places to brutality. The tormentors are torturers and no longer beloved parents or educators. They who punish no longer love; in fact, the reverse, they hate. *Oliver Twist* in the orphan asylums of London is no more than a miserable and panic-stricken victim (David Lean, 1947; earlier, Thomas Bentley, 1920). The young hero of *Without Family* with Robert Lynen and Joel Flateau, directed by Andre Michel in 1958, is petrified with horror at seeing the low class chief of the young thieves tie his victims to a ring and whip them, when they don't bring in enough loot. The *First Weapons* (Rene Wheeler, 1950) about the childhood of a young stable boy, is saturated with fear of a violent and cruel horsetrainer skillful at using on children whips that should not even be used on horses.

Apart from these more (or in the case of Wheeler, less) moving laments about the misfortunes of childhood martyrs one perceives that in the movies whipping is generally only an episode in a situation itself associated with certain themes of sadistic mythology. In the timorous and unfruitful attempt by Vadim to reconstruct the atmosphere and the customs of the nunnery of Sainte-Marie-des-Bois, actually a castle from *The Hundred and Twenty Days* the riding crop is the badge of the guardians; and one even catches a glimpse, when a door is opened and quickly shut of, a half-dressed young girl whose back is zebra-striped with lashes. But happily when the movies deal with the slavery of prisons or sailing ships, the laws of the underworld, or the customs of the past, they have something better to offer us.

The pretexts for scenes of slavery are preferably exotic, oriental, and historic, particularly classic antiquity. Noelle Adam, therefore, is whipped in the conjuring up of the Arabian Nights which offers the *Adventures of Aladdin.* Similarly in the *Adventures of Hadji* (Don Weis, 1958), *The Prodigal* (Richard Thorpe, 1955), or better still, nearer to the East, in India, the two versions of *Bengal Tiger,* Joe May, 1934 and Fritz Lang, 1958 where the hero, the victim, is even pegged between two stakes. Marisa Allasio, at the beginning of the Christian era, is a bossy servant who thrashes Gianna Maria Canale without pity, pursuing the girl, whip in hand, until she falls under the blows (*Slaves of Carthage*). If Carthage is without pity, so is its rival, Rome. To save Sylvia Sims from the dishonor ordered by Nicole Courcel, who has had her tied to a stake and is getting ready to tear off her tunic to prepare her for the whip, Louis Jourdan is obliged to apply "the old tactic of the snail" and surround the victim at the stake with a group of men, with their backs toward her, to preserve the girl's modesty (*Virgins of Rome,* Vittorio Cottafavi).

The world of prisons has a common border with that of slavery; and the whip, though more shamefully, reigns here with equal sovereignty. The first thing the young doctor sees when he enters the citadel dominated by the chief doctor (*Blood of the Vampire* Kass, 1958) is a prisoner, with a torn and bloody back, still tied to the frame where he had been whipped. In one prison where fate leads him, Paul Muni, hero of *I Am A Fugitive From a Chain Gang* (Mervyn Le Roy, 1932) is dragged into a cell by one of the brutes who acts as a guard, is tied face to the wall, and beaten with a thick band of leather fastened to a stump. Women are not spared. For Suzy Prim, *In the Kingdom of Heaven* (Julien Duvivier, 1949), it stopped at the threat, but the unfortunate females in the hulk of the *Ship of Lost Women* (Rafaello Matarazzo, 1953) are effectively lashed at every opportunity.

The navy, particularly the old navy of the sailing vessels, whose pure and hard morality is well known, made the use of the whip, even on ships not manned by impressed sailors, a favorite pastime. The cruel treatment reached its peak, of course, in the prison fleet, the galleys, where Masciste (*Pastrone,* 1914) Errol Flynn (*The Sea Hawk*), and even the three Stooges (*The Three Stooges Meet Hercules*) all suffered. The daily ration of brutality was guaranteed by the boatswain, who with a long whip always ready, paced between the benches of the rowers. The self-sacrifice of Pierre Fresnay (*Monsieur Vincent;* Maurice Cloche, 1947), given the obvious masochism of the hero he is playing, becomes very ambigu-

ous. But the ordinary ships, especially when they belong to
the fleet of Her Very Gracious British Majesty, carry officers
and boatswains willing to apply severe punishment. During
his two years as an ordinary seaman, as the title *Two Years
Before the Mast* indicates, Alan Ladd was whipped by Howard
Da Silva. The sinister commander of the "Bounty", Charles
Laughton in the first version (Frank Lloyd, 1935), Trevor
Howard in the second (Lewis Milestone, 1962) therefore
very naturally diverts himself by having a sailor guilty of a
minor offense tied to the mast and his skin cut from his back
by lashes of the whip (*Mutiny on the Bounty*). In this situation, Clark Gable, then Marlon Brando, take the justified
step of leading the mutiny. *Billy Budd,* Melville's hero played
by Terence Stamp under Peter Ustinov's direction, does not
get this chance. His private mutiny against the inhuman treatment of the navy does not lead to a haven in a Polynesian
Eden but to the hangman's rope.

The whip can become an instrument of atrocious, almost
fatal, torture. In the hands of the abominable Ku Klux Klan
it is the subject of lynching episodes, and Dick Foran suffers
greatly by it (*Black Legion,* 1937). To portray the thrashing
of the policemen in *Trial* (1962), Orson Welles directed a
sequence where the rapid montage and use of long shots, as
Ado Kyrou notes in "Positif" (No. 50-52 p. 105) gives an
abominable impression of pure suffering and brutality by
beating Anthony Perkins to the verge of fainting. In expert
hands, the long whip of the charioteer becomes a true weapon,
against which Cornel Wilde has to defend himself in *Hot
Blood* (Nicholas Ray) as does also the director and hero of
The Kentuckian, Burt Lancaster. Always ready to wound,
even to kill, the whip is, in the countries where morals are
primitive and might is right, the very symbol of power, as
the Louis Milestone movie, *The Law of the Whip* demonstrates

in a modern survival where geographic remoteness justifies the anachronism of medieval customs. Note, for example, the various tortures of Quasimodo in the different versions of *The Hunchback of Notre Dame* that permitted Charles Laughton, as well as Anthony Quinn, to writhe in their chains under the savage lashes of the leather wielded by the torturer.

If one does succeed in separating the ambiguous link between the whip and sensuality, it returns very quickly. The movies offer a complete embellishment for this type of amorous relation: from the normal (if one may call it that) heterosexual, to the pathological (as nearly as one dares to write), homosexual, and even to the symbolic. Jules Berry at the end of *Visitors of the Evening,* like Xerxes wishing to avenge himself on the sea, uses his riding crop to flail at inanimate objects and statues (Marcel Carne, 1942).

The man who whips a woman is generally, and at first *always,* presented as a barbarian. Their morals are those of the ferocious guerrillas of Pancho Villa (*Viva Villa,* Jack Conway, 1934). The Eskimo of *Frozen Justice* who with a sealskin thong beats Lenore Ulric fallen at his feet, is the northern brother of these Mexicans. In savage lands, therefore, women must often have recourse to the method used by Gladys Walton, who in *The Girl Who Ran Wild,* is compelled to flourish a revolver to make the massive and bearded beast who threatens her with his whip keep a respectful distance. Today, these are the customs of the underworld toughs, and the "wives" of these gentlemen just have to comply with them. Moreover they know and, at least passively, accept their fate. When, in *Rififi* (Jules Dassin, 1954), Marie Sabouret sees Jean Servais, whom she has deceived while he was in prison, take off his belt, she does not make a single gesture of revolt, nor even try to exonerate herself; she undoes the buttons of her dress to bare her back. Similarly, with the heroine of

Orient Night. And is echoed in the shot that parodies this, in *Holiday for Henrietta* where, stretched on her bed, the woman watches, with a mixture of fear and desire, as the man approaches her, whip in hand. In the underworld, the whip is always a good way to soften the flesh, and get the innocent victims of white slavery on the move (*Missing Women,* Edward Molinaro, 1958) and (*Despise Yourselves Little Girls,* Yves Allegret, 1957) who are, one gathers, even less disposed than the regulars to accept without complaint this strict rule. Aided by such good examples, the contemporary whip goes beyond these sociological works and Maxwell Reed can be seen horsewhipping Patricia Rokin, *The Brothers* (David MacDonald, 1947); and Francoise Arnould is similarly punished in *The Lovers of Tage* (Henri Verneuil, 1953). The whip finds its original function again in being the passageway to other cruelties. The historic Italian film *The Castle of Evil Loves* (Riccardo Freda), where Gino Gervi flagellates Mirielle Granelli in a scene whose incestuous undertones are very clearly drawn, finds its logical outcome in Mario Camerini's film, *Ulysses* (1953) where the unfaithful concubines of the king of Ithaca are not only whipped, but once even pinned to the wall by a lance thrown by Telemachus, Franco Interlenghi.

Sometimes, doubtlessly a little weary of being beaten, it happens that women reverse the roles. In this case, the pretexts are much more tenuous. To the masculine masochists and the feminine sadists for whom these scenes are intended, the productions offer a particularly stereotyped construction. First as to costume, almost always the same: the women are constantly wearing high boots and carrying riding crops. It would be rather naive to believe that it is pure coincidence when one sees that the scriptwriter of *The Young Wolves* and its producer, Michael Anderson (1958) chose, for settling accounts between Susan Kohner and Robert Wagner, the very moment when not only is the young man naked to the waist, but the heroine is in a riding habit.

Chance had very little to do with it when the publicity of *The Counterfeit Traitor* heavily stressed the riding clothes of the sex kitten, Ingrid von Bergan whose Germanic name is not a negligible added attraction in calling to mind Aurora Von Rumelin, alias Wanda Von Dunajav, alias all Leopold Sacher-Masoch heroines. This is an instance where pretexts are as slender as they are no longer timely. And as for grab-bags, nothing could be more uneven than *Carrousel Napolitain* (by Ettore Giannini, 1952); one scene is, in this respect, particularly astonishing in being the evocation of an erotic photograph. Sophia Loren, in black underwear, whip in hand, poses for the photographer. At her side, on all fours, is a gentleman with a moustache whose suit evokes La Belle Epoque (1890's). On all fours, or crawling along the ground, is similarly the posture Stanley Baker adopts before Jeanne Moreau when she beats him in *Eva* (Joseph Losey, 1962); a film in which other conformities with Sacher-Masoch have been raised, particularly by Fereydoun Hoveyda: "The introduction of the character of the shipowner (Greek) recalls "Venus in Furs": the heroine . . . leaves her husband for a Greek". Less intellectualized, but perhaps the more wildly sensual is the daughter of Fu Manchu, Fah-Lo-See (Myrna Loy) who after Terry (Charles Starett) has been whipped, amorously licks the wounds of her lover in *The Mask of Fu Manchu* (Charles Brabin, 1932). Feminine aggressiveness manifests itself as well, perhaps better, in the area of homosexuality and is only the more exhilarating for the viewer, especially the male. The famous scene in *Queen Kelly* (1928) where the queen pursues Gloria Swanson all through her palace, whipping her along the corridors and grand stairways

under the impassive eyes of the sentries, not only reveals
some of Stroheim's tastes, (discernible, for example, at the
beginning of *Merry-go-Round* (1922) although, there on a
heterosexual theme), but remains the major attraction in
the movie. These little sessions may be instructional, helping
us to understand the threats of the piano teacher in *The
Seventh Veil* (Compton Bennet, 1946) or, better still, they
may be domestic. To compel Gina Lollobrigida to marry a
man she rejects, all the women in the household combine to
spread her out on a table and whip her without mercy (*The
Law*, Jules Dassin). Jean Gabin's mother uses a similar pretext to whip Danielle Delorme in *The Time of the Killers*
(Julien Duvivier, 1956). Elsewhere, two adversaries struggle
with matched weapons; in *Under the Bridge of Sighs* it is
cold steel with which Maria Frau and Luciana Vedovelli
confront each other; and cold steel also in *Mam'zelle Bona-
parte* (Christian-Jaque, 1941), but it is horsewhips with which
Christine Nordeu and Bery Baxter are armed in *Idol of Paris*
(Leslie Arliss, 1947). And quite naturally we arrive at the
suggestive tableau offered by Nadine Tallier in a white, slit
dress turning over, every way, on a bed covered with (of
course) white fur, in order to escape the cuts of the lash with
which Juliette Greco, swelling out a tight-fitting black dress,
is beating her, in her rage. It would be difficult to epitomize
flagellation between women better than with this astonishing
scene, in an otherwise mediocre film by Raoul Andre (*Man
and Child*, 1957).

The most perfidiously pederastic scenes of flagellation between men are not always those which declare themselves
explicitly. When in Reme Clement's *The Demand* (1947),
aboard a submarine which is transporting Nazis to Argentina,
a Gestapo chief unbuckles his belt to strike Michael Auclair,
the cards are not stacked. Nothing in this situation is hidden:

we are expressly told it's an aunty and her lover boy, and, moreover, that this is a typical situation for mature men of status and virility. When in *Scheherazade* one sees a man plunged into a harem swimming pool among the naked odalisques, and beaten from the edge by a eunuch, the situation becomes a little more complicated. When Marlon Brando in (*One-Eyed Jacks,* 1957), the first film he directed himself, profits from this opportunity by having himself tied and whipped for long minutes by Karl Malden, the circumstances become even less clear. But the richest measure of such ambiguity, the situation where an otherwise very strong will appears to change, is offered in two of Burt Lancaster's movies. This actor, otherwise talented and agreeable, prides himself on having received, in the making of *Kiss the Blood Off My Hands* (Norman Foster, 1948) real lashes from an authentic cat-o'-nine-tails for the purpose, of course, of getting himself perfectly into his role. *The Rope of Sand* (William Dieterle, 1948) also offers us a truly extraordinary scene. At the beginning of the film, Lancaster, in the hands of a cruel police officer, Paul Henreid, is led into a whipping room, where whips of an admirable richness and variety decorate the walls. There he is tied to a frame, in an unbelievable position, legs apart, buttocks projecting, to receive the intended torture.

To close, let us point out that certain devotees of beatings whip themselves. A monk in *Sorcery Through the Ages* and a nun, Yvette Lebon in *Milady and the Musketeers* (Vittorio Cottafavi, 1951) do this, linking the joys of a voluntary mortification, expertly measured, to the fascination of solitary pleasure.

THE TORTURE CHAMBER

At the end of the line, agony meets torture. Whether or

not it is followed by death is not of direct importance here; we find ourselves at a completely different level than that of the picturesque, sometimes cruel, deaths which we have already inventoried. Here, in truth, the mechanical outshines the accidental or the spectacular; the agony need no longer depend on a completely superficial motivation, better designed to titivate rather than really to seduce. A certain quality of suffering is all that counts, obtained with the aid of a technique that has its classic instruments, among which the whip has already played a part, but which leaves the field free for more astonishing inventions.

The surest way to guide ourselves, like a new Clara, in this new torture chamber along paths that lead to episodes—some the exact evocations of the Chinese inventions which Mirbeau described, but numerous others that contribute new refinements — is again, to proceed by categories.

ACID, BURNING WAX, MOLTEN LEAD, BOILING OIL. One of the most ravishing episodes in the very rich *Colossus of Rhodes* (Sergio Grieco, 1960) is the spectacle that gives us a bare-chested athlete, tied horizontally, and on whose chest falls, drop by drop, an unspecified but definitely corrosive substance, as proved by the little clouds of vapor which, to the rhythm of the dripping, rise from the victim's skin.

Acid is also used in a more brutal fashion; a full bowl of vitriol which, when it misses its human target, instantly dissolves the innocent placard it hits. This is what happens in *The Thirst of Evil* by Orson Welles. In *Party Girl* (Nicholas Ray, 1960), Lee J. Cobb has the dreadful urge to disfigure Cyd Charisse with a jar of vitriol, under the eyes of the man who loves her, Robert Taylor.

The droplets and the bowlful may seem a little timid, if we consider the spectacular results made possible by the use of a swimming pool. Pursued by a diabolically animated skeleton, a woman dressed (an additional refinement) in a long nightgown backs away without watching her feet — and falls into tank that is immediately agitated by a sinister bubbling (*The Night of All Mysteries,* William Castle). Or better still, a human body is tied with a uncorrodible chain then plunged, by an ingenious arrangement of pulleys, into a cistern and finally, after the effervescence, up comes the perfectly clean skeleton (*Crime in the Museum of Horrors,* Arthur Crabtree, 1958).

Several variants of these tanks will be examined later, in the paragraph on "burning pits".

In a more primitive form (physical rather than chemical), boiling oil, burning pitch, and melted lead, scalding liquids in general, were war weapons highly prized in the Middle Ages. These ingredients are rediscovered in countless sieges in medieval films. In Fleming's *Joan of Arc* for example, (a film whose sadistic richness can be endlessly discussed), and with greater frenzy and romanticism in the various versions of *The Hunchback of Notre Dame* where the famous episode of Quasimodo causing a torrent of fire to flow from the gargoyles of the cathedral manages to lift to an honorable level even the flattest and most pallid adaptations of Victor Hugo's marvellous book, that by Jean Delannoy for example.

ANIMALS—When it comes to torture the most inventive animals are, without doubt, insects. The maggots that fill the glass caskets of Ray Milland in *Premature Burial* (Roger Corman) are not the only generators of moral torments, frantic anguish and stomach-turning disgust; for under the inordinately long-nailed fingers of the sinister Doctor Fu Manchu, spiders and scorpions become the skillful tormentors of Lawrence Grant in *The Mask of Fu Manchu* (1938). And what of Sean Connery's emotions when, playing the government killer, James Bond, a tickling wakes him to see an enormous black widow spider (treacherously introduced into his hotel room by the maleficent Dr. No) walking across him! He knows that the least movement that may frighten the creature would trigger a fatal defensive reflex; and he must, therefore, lying completely immobile, witness the promenade of the horrid beast across his chest, before being free to crush it when it leaves his skin for the pillow case (*Dr. No,* Terence Young, 1962). The spider can (like the carnivores cited earlier in our short dictionary of the less common deaths) even become an eater of men. Giant in size, it devours the sailors whom the mammoth gorilla has thrown into the abyss, in a scene from *King Kong.* This alas, was cut from the final version by the authors themselves. In natural size, a garden spider swallows a fly that, by a perverse trick of foolhardy science, has in an unforeseen mixup acquired the human chest and head of the unfortunate experimentor (*The Fly*). When raised to giant-size by some scientific device, insects show themselves to be even more destructive, and enormously more terrifying. The most successful, the best made, and therefore the one in which the cruelty and apprehension are most extreme, is *Them* by Gordon Douglas, who with great talent directs the giant ants, stridulant in the sandstorms. Jack Arnold substitutes a tarantula of proportionally increased size for the ants (*Tarantula,* 1955), and Nathan Juran a gigantic praying mantis (*The Deadly Mantis,* 1956). Fruits of experiments by Captain Nemo, who thought to find in them a remedy for the world's hunger, are the grotesquely oversized crabs, chickens and bees in *The Mysterious Island* (Cyril Enfield, 1960).

In a scene, cut (but most likely by a modest distributor) from the same James Bond movie, but brought to the attention of movie-lovers by the ever-alert Pierre Philippe ("Cinema 63", no. 76, p. 79), Ursula Andress, fastened to the ground and sexily disrobed, is delivered to the appetite of hungry crabs. Fear itself as Vincent Price discovers, in the course of his hideous experiments in which he racks his brains for ways to terrify his subjects, is nothing other than an enormous larva which clutches at the spinal column of the terrified (*The Tingler,* William Castle).

Finally, insects devour each other in the course of totally inhuman struggles, in which, jointed or viscous, they use weapons which sever, pierce or paralyze with a virtuosity that one would have believed reserved for the inhabitants of the second or third planet of Alpha Centaurus. *The Sand of Death* (Zgourdi) as well as *Fresh Water Killers* recounts episodes of these, on the whole, genuinely terrifying battles.

By comparison with such varied and subtle skills, vertebrates are at a great disadvantage. Reduced to such broad strokes as the elephant head-crusher called the "bird fly" of *The Five Sous of Lavarede,* or the goat licking the feet of *Francis the First* (Christian Jaques), or to the sentimental tale, such as the cobra killer of the little boy in *The River* (Jean Renoir), these beasts have only trifling opportunities to show their capacities. One is grateful to Alfred Hitchcock for giving the birds their revenge; not just the illusions of madness as in *Franju,* but the very enactment of madness which plucks out eyes and tears human beings to bits, with a strong preference for children (*The Birds,* 1962). Having witnessed a murder, the animal can become a terrifying agent of justice, driving the guilty to madness (*The Shadow of the Cat,* John Gilling).

THE BELL—Octave Mirbeau has described in detail the torture of the bell. You enclose your victim in an adequate-sized bronze bell, and you bang on the side of this bell with regularity and vigor. Very soon the victim, eardrums shattered and body semi-liquified by the vibrations, is in the exact state of physical and moral decomposition that you aimed for. Fu Manchu subjected Sir Lionel Barton to this torture, and it is found again in *Colossus of Rhodes;* and also in *Fantomas* by Feuillade, with a variation in which the victim, hanging by his feet, takes the place of the clapper.

Modernized, the torture of the bell becomes, in *The Big Congo* (J. Lewis, 1955), electronic. In bringing the volume of a Sonotone up to full strength, one gets an equivalent result with an apparatus that is much simpler to obtain.

Conversely, it is then possible to cut a deaf person off from the world of sound by pulling out the wires of his hearing aid, a reverse process but surely as cruel as attempts, by blows, to make the mute Harpo Marx talk (*Love Happy,* David Miller).

CHILDREN—Childhood, as scientifically understood today after a half-century of psychopathology, is in no way the age of sweetness and innocence. The moment comes when the adult can do no more than to approve the vengeful cry of the rough Alfred: "Destroy that Child!"

In contrast to the abominable Joselito, there is the fearful and believable kid who flabbergasted and terrorized W. C. Fields, as a bank guard (*Never Give a Sucker an Even Break*); Fields, in all his films, keeps a sharp fang ready for the delicious little babes because of his realistic knowledge of their clever evil-mindedness. There is Hal Roach's *Our Gang* series. There is the calculated madness of *Dennis the Menace,* a comic strip by Hank Ketchum, adapted for television by Charles Barton. There is *Little Iodine,* cited in the chapter on spanking. There is Shirley Temple who in the course of a tearjerker tranquilly begins to tear apart her dolls. There is her barely-elder sister Jean Seberg the heroine of *Bonjour Tristesse* by Otto Preminger, who sticks pins in her dolls with deliberate voodoo intent. Children actually terrorize gangsters who are foolhardy enough to kidnap them, to the great joy of their parents who refuse to have their progeny returned, even for free (*Ransom of Red Chief*).

Hitchcock's distaste for nymphettes in glasses, whom he persists in killing off throughout the history of his movies, and who all have the face of his daughter, Patricia, is self-explanatory. He knows perfectly well that these little girls, just at the awkward age, are the sisters of the wild students of St. Trinian. He knows that his colleague, Mervyn Le Roy in *The Bad Seed* has recounted the career of a ravishing little blonde who is raised to be a truly gifted killer. And the indignation some viewers feel at this portrayal of reality, I am sure, is more the reaction of panic at the brutal truth than resentment of a falsification.

Who will one day dare to produce Ray Bradbury's "Little Killer"?

HELL—The threat of eternal torments exists in the dogmas of virtually every religion, constituting one of their most delightful doctrines. Who, looking at the triptych in the Prado, would tarry over the panel showing the abode of bliss? The Elysian Fields are pallid beside Tartarus who has become a synomyn for all of Hell. Preachers find themselves much more successful in depicting scenes of eternal torment than in painting future bliss.

The strictly Christian inspiration in the movies scarcely attains the level of this lyricism. The devils are good devils, sometimes burlesqued as in *Hellzapoppin,* and their ovens turn only moderately red. The Prince of Shadows in Lubitsch, as well as in Minnelli and Bergman, is a very debonaire tyrant and a rather weary executioner.

Dante and mythology fortunately come to the aid of these insipidities. *The Inferno,* by Giuseppe de Liguoro, as well as that by Lachman, borrows its design from the best source,

Gustave Dore. *Masciste in Hell* (Brignone) shows devils knowledgably torturing charmingly undressed damned girls. Hercules in *Hercules Meets the Vampires,* under the expert direction of Mario Bava (1961), encounters several famous and picturesque damned souls: Ixion, Tantalus, Sysiphus and, bizarrely, Prometheus. Masciste himself, guided by Riccardo Freda, has the same classical encounters, although the theme of the second *Masciste in Hell* (1963), is clearly a Christian inspiration. It bears witness that myths come to each others' aid.

But what Moslem movie-maker will dare to tell us in contrast, of the magnificently spectacular delights in Allah's paradise? Whatever the merits of *Sinners in Hell,* a Japanese film by Nuobo Nakagawa may prove to be (it is known only by hearsay in France (in 1961)), we are entitled to expect a little novelty from that land.

BRANDING IRON—The branding iron is basically the instrument for marking livestock, and hence finds a place in numerous Westerns from *My Darling Clementine* (John Ford), to *The Implacable Ones* (Raoul Walsh), to *Cowboy* (Delmer Davis), and *Red River* (Howard Hawkes).

Diverted from its primary function it is an instrument as painful as it is humiliating when used to brand slaves and convicts. After having been sent to a terrifying prison, Errol Flynn, tied to a post, finds himself branded on the shoulder (*Captain Blood,* Michael Curtis). In the various versions of *The Three Musketeers* Milady is branded by the executioner of Bethune.

Similarly a man brands the woman who has become his thing. The bandits of *O'Cangaceiro* do this, and so does Sessue Hayakawa in *The Cheat* (Cecil B. Demille, 1915).

The white-hot knife that blinds Michael Strogoff is an interesting variant of the branding iron.

BURNING PITS—In one of the most fascinating episodes of *The Prodigal* (Richard Thorpe), a pretty adolescent, under the impassive eye of Lana Turner, plunges into a basin of fire. The theme of the burning pit, homage, at minimum, to its beauty, turns up again in many other films and, of course, in all the films about Hell; but also in *The Body Snatcher* (Robert Wise, 1945) and its remake by John Gilling, *The Flesh and the Fiends,* 1959.

Frankenstein (James Whale, 1935), and many of its remakes, traditionally have the scorching and sulphurous pit as the only way to destroy the monster. Burning materials are actually very diverse, since they range from liquid wax, in the two versions of *The Cabinet of Wax Figures,* to radioactive liquid in *Dr. No,* by which the sinister savant meets his poetically just end.

THE MIDDLE AGES—A complete nomenclature of all the instruments, used by justice up to the Eighteenth Century, to discover truth, requires an erudition which is unfortunately foreign to us and which keeps us from setting down the correct names for the spiked machines, various pincers and pulleys which, when brought out and set in motion, even in a dry-run terrified *Joan of Arc,* Dreyer (1928). These instruments, or their brothers, turn up in *Dies Irae* by the same author. In the various versions of *Hunchback of Notre Dame* found in cinema history, Esmeralda undergoes the classic torture of the boot which, as we know, essentially consists in imprisoning the legs of the victim, even when she is Gina Lollabrigida, between two planks and driving the wedge between these planks until the bones break.

Although less horrible, the water torture could hardly be less distressing, unless one acted like Fernandel in *Francis the First,* and bribed the torturers to substitute wine for water.

It is necessary to remember that judicial torture has not

disappeared with the Dark Ages. We have already spoken of the common working-over, but with the war in Algeria other, more scientific, methods were utilized by the intelligence agencies of the French army. Jean-Luc Godard did not intend to miss such a windfall. The bath and electricity, "the shower-head" and the wet towel are described in *The Little Soldier* (1959), with a stylish contempt for the biases of (let us say) the left — though now attributed to the F.L.N. Skillful publicity carefully rumored that the actor, Michel Subor, had been, for the sake of verisimilitude "twenty-four times a second" actually subjected to electric shocks. Admirable integrity on the part of the producer, and splendid professional conscience.

WALLS—Edgar Allen Poe's novel "The Pit and the Pendulum" set a fashion for movable walls which come together in order to crush. They are of course found again in the adaptations of this novella (Roger Corman and Edward Abrahams) but also in *The Raven* (Louis Friedlander, 1935). The hero of this admirable film, Bela Lugosi, corrupted by too passionate a reading of Edgar Allen Poe, has the mechanisms of the book reconstructed and at the denouement is himself crushed by the walls of bronze.

Let us cite two other variants. The panels, equipped with spikes of steel, which are forced to meet, piercing and crushing their victim simultaneously, in *The Mask of Fu Manchu,* and the wall, embellished with sharpened knives, in *Buccaneer of the Islands.*

PENDULUM—As with the walls, the pendulum finds its place of honor in the three films by Corman, Abrahams and Friedlander that were inspired by Poe.

PINCERS; TONGS—Tongs, sometimes used glowing redhot, and previously noted in the Inquisition's arsenal, appear occasionally in more contemporary circumstances. At the beginning of

In High Gear by Robert Aldrich, some killers torture a young woman to death. Although the body of the tortured girl is outside the shot (only her legs are seen) the torture instruments cross the screen. Among these is a pair of pincers. Tongs were also represented as part of the arsenal of the Gestapo torturing Marcello Pagliero in Rossellini's *Open City.*

When the hardware stores are closed or too far away, a minimum of inventiveness allows one to compensate for this. For example, it is sufficient to wedge the victim's hand in a drawer upon which one leans a little harder when it is necessary to make him talk (*In High Gear*). A door does the business as well, and Pierre Batcheff thus has his wrist trapped in *An Andalusian Dog* (Luis Bunuel).

Since the points of ice-tong jaws are sharpened to assure a better grip, they allow for a double and simultaneous perforation. It suffices to place the points on opposite sides of the victim's neck, and shut the jaws with a sharp snap.

PUNCTURES—The maniac of the puncture, his needle skillfully held, directed towards the most fleshy portions of his female neighbors is a familiar figure on public transportation. This amateur can, at the movies, admire his colleagues, and actually find examples and ideas.

In the first *Masciste in Hell,* the favorite pleasure of the demons was to prick the beautiful, damned women with their forks, but they operate a little haphazardly, lacking the methodicalness, without which esthetics is impossible. The true pricker favors one part of the body, generally the buttocks, or better, as with Caussimon in Edmond T. Greville's *Port of Desire,* the breasts. Technique also becomes perfected. There is perceptible progress from the needle point guided towards the eye, by the hand already cited from *Immediate Action,* to the ingenious artfulness of *Crime in the Museum of Horrors.*

Points are concealed in binoculars, held in position by a spring which slackens when the knob is adjusted, thus activating them. There are those who like to set fire to splinters which they slide under the fingernails; for example, those of Gary Cooper in *Lives of a Bengal Lancer* (Henry Hathaway, 1935); and the little flames, reflected in the varnish of the table, give a very pretty Christmas tree effect. Oriental science comes to the rescue of occidental technique. In *Terror of the Tongs* (Anthony Bushell) the sinister chief of the Chinese bandits, played by Christopher Lee, utilizes the cooperation of a professional acupuncter. With the help of an extremely fine needle that leaves no visible trace, the practitioner of this art, aided by his specialist's familiarity with very sensitive spots, can induce unspeakable suffering in those he tortures.

Points are also used as accessories of more or less complex machines. The Nuremberg Bride, that sinister sarcophagus in the shape of a woman's body which, when shut, perforates those it encloses, appears in *He Who Laughs* (L'Homme qui rit) by Paul Leni (1928). The inside of a bronze mask is similarly spiked in *The Mask of the Demon* (Mario Bava, 1960) before being fitted, with a sledgehammer, to the face of a witch or warlock. A spiked roller designed to be towed by horses, is, in an unforeseen mischance, dragged over the outstretched body of a Negro (*The Titans,* Duccio Tessari, 1961).

We cannot close without citing the dagger camera tripod of Michael Powell's *The Peeper* (1960).

Sexual Assassins and Vampires

In contrast to both the calculating assassin, the cold blooded hero of *A Kiss Before Dying* who kills without pleasure, simply to satisfy his ambition, and the unconscious brute incapable of making a distinction between love and rape, between caressing and crushing, like Lenny in Lewis Milestone's *Of Mice and Men* (1939) there is the killer for pleasure, in whom enjoyment can fully flower only in the death of the loved being.

The primary impulses of the *Sadist of the Highway* (*Sadique de l'autoroute*), like the monstrous and brutal thirsts of *I Was a Teenage Frankenstein,* which preeminently consist in the various joys of a crime executed on the run, are only resonances, weak echoes of two great myths, which, like all self-respecting myths, have a solid basis in reality.

The first, in chronological order, is the myth of Jack the Ripper. At the beginning of the century, in the sordid fog-clouded side streets of London's East End, prostitutes were found horribly mutilated by a criminal who opened their abdomen with a single accurate stroke of his blade. Despite all the efforts of the police to capture him, the Ripper, who was even offered the charming temptation of bobbies dressed as women, could never be captured. He disappeared one fine day, unpunished; and we are reduced to guesswork as to his identity.

Then, helped by the movies, the myth began. Alfred Hitchcock's intention in *The Lodger* (1926) at the outset, is ingenious enough. The action of his movie, disdaining the macabre episode, is centered on suspicion. The innocent lodger, a worthy fellow, from his inexplicable absences leads one to wonder is he not in fact the murderer of the prostitutes? Unfortunately, the concept deteriorates through the course of the production that is rich in childish effects (where glass ceilings allow the audience to imagine the penetrating sound of the suspect's pacing in his room, and that is completely solemn in perfectly ridiculous scenes (when pursued by an inevitably stupid crowd, the hero, obviously innocent, is

likened, by a very explicit shot, to Christ nailed to the cross).
Two years later, fortunately, G. W. Pabst's *Loulou,* which I
personally maintain is the most beautiful film in the history
of the movies, managed to erase the shadow of this dreary
"good lordishness". Louise Brooks, fallen to the lowest depths,
but more marvelously beautiful than ever, wanders in foggy
streets. She meets a young man, solemn and sad, and takes
him to her room. The young man is Jack the Ripper, and, in
the course of a scene which is the most splendid and sacri-
legious example of a strictly wordly "transfiguration", he is
stunned by the beauty of his victim. It is only much later
that his madness gets the upper hand. Let us note for the
record, even though we have not seen it, *The Avenger* (also
entitled *Murders*) 1934, with the beautiful Elisabeth Allen
and Ivor Novello; and the very expressionistic *The Lodger*
(John Brahm, 1944) where, contrasted with Hitchcock's film,
the lodger, loved by Merle Oberon, is really the killer; and
let us come to the incontestable masterpiece of the genre:
Jack the Ripper, by Monty Berman and Robert S. Baker,
excellently interpreted by Lee Paterson and Eddie Byrne
(1959). The admirable London of the 90's was their pretext
for a minutely detailed evocation, where fog, smoke and
dripping were extensively fermented to encourage spontaneous
generation of horror. The sordid slums, peopled with girls
more or less undressed, in the various versions have nothing
over the disturbing middle-class house whose Victorian re-
spectability was rife with the most terrifying possibilities.
Even the solution to the enigma, as proposed by Baker and
Berman, was very plausible. Jack the Ripper was a surgeon
devoted to purity; hence the clinical skillfulness of the murderer — and his bitterness.

Some twenty years later, during the so-called crazy years,
Germany succeeded the United Kingdom as the haunt of

crazy murderers. The Vampire of Dusseldorf overshadows the
London disembowler. Fritz Lang's *M* (1931) drew inspiration
from his exploits. A timid and unobtrusive petty employee,
Peter Lorre, surrenders to his favorite pastime: dragging little
girls into an out-of-the-way corner, and gutting them. Lang's
genius made *M* a film in which the presence of death was
heavy in each shot, including the ghastly face of the hero.
One of the victims, in what is possibly the most famous of
these shots, just comes into sight through a shop window, in
which is reflected a complete assortment of knives that Peter
Lorre is contemplating with undisguised interest. All these
objects, and a child's balloon, surround him with a halo of
evil. The virtues of the remake, in 1949 by Joseph Losey,
are at least equivalent even though the American approach
dwells more on terror; since, in order to conceal its banality,
it is possibly more subtle than the all too-explicitly expressionistic German approach. Both drew an identical lesson
from the macabre tale. In the face of the impotence of the
police, whose frenzied, reckless and ineffective investigation
is endangering its existence, the underworld, suddenly en-
amored of virtue, decides to tackle the problem itself. The
thieves succeed where the law had failed; but the author of
The Lawless as well as that of *Fury,* sided with law against
lynching, while conceding extenuating circumstances of mental
illness to the criminal.

The sexual crime whose shadow hovers over the environs
of *Hangover Square* (John Brahm, 1945) where Laird Cregar
takes the role of a mad criminal, promises, in addition, the
most sinister discoveries to those who wish to unveil them.
Boris Karloff, a novelist, is vitally interested in a strange
criminal affair. Young women have been strangled, then mutilated by scalpel-cuts. Their murderer has protested his innocence to the very gallows. The truth that the amateur detective

finally discovers is infinitely horrible to him. He himself is really the guilty one; and at contact with the fatal scalpel his instinctual drives, which had been blocked by amnesia, regain their force and he begins to kill again (*Grip of the Strangler*, Robert Day, 1958).

The knife itself, weapon par excellence for such murders, sometimes becomes superfluous. After strangling their shared friend with a rope, the two pederasts of Alfred Hitchcock's *Rope* (1948) recall with sensual delight the risks of their crime. *The Sniper* (Edward Dmytryck (1952), shows a criminal who shoots amorous couples with a rifle that has a telescopic lens, joining the pleasures of the voyeur to the more robust joys of murder. Despite a socially unpleasant content — *The Sniper* wanted to vindicate police confessions, a particular sordid justifying — Dmytryck's film has, in the history of the cinema, at least one virtue. It is like an outline for that masterpiece, perfect in every respect, *The Peeper* (Michael Powell, 1960).

Better know as Presburger's associate, in cooperation with whom he made the best, *A Matter of Life and Death,* and the less good, *Tales of Hoffman,* Powell planned to depict an exceptional case of psychopathia sexualis. His hero, Karl-Heinz Boehm, with the good face of the healthy sports hero, has, as his besetting sin, an obsession to film death. He installs a miniature darkroom in his house to develop those films which it would be difficult to send to Kodak; and with his Bell-Howell in hand he wanders the streets, on the lookout for a beautiful accident or an attractive sudden death. Female victims are evidently his preference, and when he finds himself short of news he becomes a director and creates truth in his own movie. His material is craftily conceived for this purpose: one leg of his tripod conceals a sharp-edged dagger; so efficiently, that a single zoom can record the terror of death and the jerks of the victim on film, as the knife plunges into his throat. Pushing professional conscience to the outer limits, he applies himself to staging his deed, and, for example, in filming the discovery of a crime which he has committed, takes every risk. Here is one who, as a commentary of the movies on itself, largely defeats the purpose of Lang in *Fury* or (TV movies) *The Diabolical Dr. Mabuse*.

For the pleasure of crime is intimately linked to the fascination with death. The taste for the morbid in the movies is almost as old as the marvels of its techniques. The love goddesses made it the favorite background of their decadent adventures. Theda Bara, archetype of the "Vamp" (for vampire), had taken (a little after Pina Minichelli and her sisters), as her name the anagram of "arab death". She took great pleasure in the presence of coffins, funeral trappings, and (unexpected resurgence of the favorite figures of the Danse Macabre) the skeleton.

The English resurrectionists were more scientifically inclined in that Belle Epoque so cordial to the abnormal. Robert Wise, (whose role, parenthetically, in the genesis of the new school of horror film is still scandalously unknown, and to whose renown a little of the eulogy which is lavished on the English school should really reflect), was, to my knowledge, the first to paint their exploits. Boris Karloff, under his direction, played a grave robber in *The Body Snatcher*. He desecrated graves and stole freshly-buried corpses to provide Henry Daniell with material for his dissection lectures. Punished in the very manner of his own crimes (when vigilant patrols were set up near the cemeteries, he turned killer to continue to provide his wares) he is killed and dissected, in his turn, by the doctor who ends up losing his mind and killing himself. The remake by John Gilling, *The Flesh and the Fiends,* is in no way unworthy of, and often even surpasses, its model.

The dealers in corpses are, in this version, two pals who prove unequalled when they find it necessary to choke, with a delight completely free of any scruple, an old beggar lady.

Let us admit a recollection from *Colossus of Rhodes* where a scene of amorous pursuit is spiced by unfolding itself in subterranean caverns decorated with dusty mummies; and let us come then to the perfect example of the genre, which is *The Abominable Doctor Hichcock* (without the "t") alias, *Raptus,* signed Robert Hampton, a pseudonym — the little story is certainly by Riccardo Freda (1962). From the start, this film concentrates on dispelling any uncertainty. In the foggy night of a nocturnal cemetery, a gravedigger finishes excavating a tomb. A shadow glides behind him, fells him, turns to the coffin lying on the ground, opens it and stares with amazement at the beautiful dead girl lying in it. Then he lies down on her. The hero, again a talented surgeon, has (elsewhere) perfected a remarkable anesthetic which confers all the appearances of a corpse on those to whom it is administered. With the help of this drug, the surgeon has worked out a strange ritual with his willing wife. He returns home late from a hard day at the hospital, and, without delay, has a governess accomplice summon his wife from the mundane routine of a musical soiree which is boring her. The guests discreetly withdraw. Radiant with anticipated joy, Marriet White joins Robert Flemyng in a room completely lined with mortuary furnishings, decorated with funeral accessories, in the center of which rises a catafalque bed surrounded by four silver candelabras. She spreads out on it; her husband approaches, makes an intravenous injection and censorship imposes the necessary skipping. Morality keeps its vigil! Led to increasing the dose for the greater satisfaction of his mania, the surgeon kills his wife. From this point the film falls into an admirable madness. Flemyng, to forget, takes flight and marries the beautiful and innocent Barbara Steele; but finds himself irresistibly drawn back to the scene of his past pleasures where, in a park transformed into a jungle, a hideous, corpselike creature prowls about on stormy nights. After having tried to kill his young wife by slitting her throat, while she is hanging upside down by her feet, the surgeon and the monster perish in flames.

Gerard Legrand in reference to this film wrote in "Positif" (No. 53, page 88): "Going beyond the threshold of parody suggested by the title, which very shrewdly criticizes itself (the obligatory view of the hand resting on the shoulder is a long shot that merely provokes a smile at the heroine's emotion), *Raptus* seems a hymn to necrophilia, whose heroine is once again named Margherita: the storms, the excessiveness, the veneer of a modern surgical decor against a stylized rococo background, and even the photography dominated by bewitching and artificial flashes of color (cf. *The Castle of Accursed Lovers*), everything warns us that British "good taste", the "disquieting" game of Terence Fisher's characters is irrelevant here. Again, not one psycho-scientific explanation comes in opposition to this outburst of mysterious passion of a type that is more nightmarish than morbid." In any case we are far from Charles Vanel's scruples who, in *Obsession* (Maurice Tourneur, 1934), was obsessed with the idea of turning Louise Lagrange into a corpse, but at the moment of strangling her had a burst of lucidity and decided to have himself committed to a mental hospital.

If Flemyng hangs Barbara Steele by the feet before trying to cut her throat, it is to collect her blood and bring back, by transfusion, the beauty of an abominably withered Marriet White. This belief in the vivifying virtues of young blood is certainly not at all new, and Freda himself in *The Vampire* made great use of it. To combat old age, the heroine lures

innocent virgins into her town house in the Marais quarter
of Paris and drains their blood before walling up their dried-
out bodies. The miracle, if it is effectively achieved, unfortunately lasts for only a limited time and the unhappy woman,
to keep intact her beauty and the love it inspires, finds herself
compelled to multiply her murders until the day, when tracked
down, she ages visibly under the horrified eyes of her pursuers.
The American equivalent to Freda, who had never had the
luck of seing his ageing stopped by a psychological shock, like
his sister in *Drums Along the Amazon,* had learned another
technique from a savage tribe. This involves a skillful blow
against the base of the skull, with a ring spiked with a kind
of dart, to collect, for drinking, the blood from the pineal
gland of a young subject (*The Leech Woman,* Edward Dein).

To every master, his due honor. Blood, the source of life,
and its cult have shadowy aristocrats who raise the trivial
necessities of nourishment to the level of metaphysical thirst.
These aristocrats of hunger are the vampires.

The belief that the dead, or at least some among them, are
vampires, is an ancient one. We do not intend to retrace the
history of Gaul and to provide an exegesis on Don Calmet.
But, limiting ourselves to the cinema, we must state that the
vampire, who today has established conventions and desires,
owes this victory of scientific reality over old wives' tales
to the vigorous works of Sheridan Le Fanu, *Carmilla,* and
above all, Bram Stoker's *Dracula,* and *I Am a Legend,* by
Richard Matheson, who really has been too rarely utilized.
Thanks to them, the fantasy of the storyteller is replaced by
an exact delineation; the vampire roams from sunset to sunrise — sometimes, according to the individual, from midnight
to three in the morning. During the day he must sleep in a
coffin filled with earth from his original tomb; he can change
himself into a wolf, mist, or bat; he is afraid of the cross,

garlic, running water and mirrors which do not reflect him; to kill him one must put a stake through his heart or expose him to the sun's rays. Lastly and above all, he has an irresistible desire for the blood of young girls, and, most importantly, the latter are irresistibly attracted to him.

In these terms, Dreyer's *Vampyr* (1930) was a perfect absurdity. To make the vampire a repulsive old woman and have her wander about at any hour of the day or night was, at the very least, a betrayal of "Carmilla", which he called his source. Le Fanu's heroine is actually, at this point, young and beautiful; and the attraction she generates is so powerful that lesbianism played a principal part in his novel. This was so evident that even Vadim, greedy for all sorts of falsification, comprehended it and made the pairing of Annette Stoyberg and Antonella Lualdi the essential driving force of his film (*And to Die of Pleasure*).

We do not propose to analyze cinematic vampirism in detail. The subject is too vast, and besides others have undertaken it, outstandingly, Jean-Claude Romer in "Vampirism in the Movies". But we must emphasize at least one point here, and that is the horrified but ecstatic submission of the victim to his executioner. As early as that often approached but never equalled archetype Murnau's *Nosferatu,* the imprudent young man and his even more willing fiancee adopt an attitude toward the monster like that of the fly toward the spider or the humming bird toward the cobra, a perhaps unconscious, but definite fascination — and we know that to enter the dwelling the vampire must be summoned from without.

The disdainful and dominating personality of Dracula responds to this eminently masochistic attitude. Bela Lugosi gave him his uniform: evening clothes, black cape, immaculate shirt front, emphasized by the bloody dash of a princely order (*Dracula,* Tod Browning, 1931). For the women, a long white tunic (*London After Midnight,* 1927 and *The Mark of the Vampire,* 1935, also by Tod Browning). The manifest signs of aristocracy finally replace the Grand Guignol and the masquerade.

Today, apart from some American efforts (that are really Mexican and Italian) vampirism has found its most qualified author in the otherwise uneven and often overestimated Terence Fisher. With *Horror of Dracula* (1958), then with *The Brides of Dracula* (1960), Fisher restored what was already lacking in *Dracula's Daughter* (Lamber Hillyer, 1936) and even more so in *The Return of the Vampire* (Lew Landers, 1943), retaining only scant traces of a lost nobility, serious-mindedness and dignity. Some were surprised not to find a trace of the humor which has been made, with Danino's help, the dominant trait of the British soul; but Fisher knew that detachment and irony are here the worst treachery. The myth is found again in its pure state in his interpretation: trans-Carpathian castle, scrupulous vampirology, bloody insistence, and, finally and preeminently, fascination.

We must agree with Michel Caen when he writes: "It is necessary to note finally this marvelous sequence, one of the most beautiful moments of post-war cinema, where Lucy Holmwood awaits the arrival of Count Dracula.

"She removes the garlic wreath, opens her window wide and rapidly takes off her cross, giving this gesture an admirable erotic significance. Then, in a swoon on the bed, quivering, breathless in her turquoise negligee, she prepares all her being to receive the fatal and delicious homage of the prince of vampires.

"It is this same Lucy who transfigured, draped in Carol Borland's winding sheet, wanders at night through bluish forests, where leaves fall in slow motion, to bring new victims to her dead lover.

"Thanks to Fisher, thanks to the *Horror of Dracula,* vampirism and the act of love are henceforth indissoluable. Death, fascination, and blood rediscover their terribly sexualized attributions, and the movies its natural right to delirium." ("Midi-Minuit Fantastique", No. 1, p. 9, 10.)

At least two other murderers must be cited in this honor role. The first is Robert Newton in Edward Dmyitryk's *Obsession.* To avenge himself on his wife's lover, Newton locks him in an underground studio and chains him up so that he can reach neither Newton himself, when the latter visits him, nor the bathtub where, day by day, Newton adds to the acid that will dissolve his body. The second is Mitchum in *Night of the Hunter,* a preacher who transforms his sermons into a hand game — on one hand is written "love", on the other "hate" — and who, to obtain money for his church, seduces, kills and robs rich widows before pursuing children in a chase that is the most exact equivalent of a nightmare as yet produced in the history of the movies.

CLASSICAL THEMES

Sadism, and this is the very essence of its romantic glamor, goes beyond the incident to its concept, awarding the place of honor to the relationships of characters among themselves, to the attitudes and, glorifying in a completely original esthetic, the locale of their encounters. This cannot be understood without the description of the lair, the castle, nor without the most primary but also the most profound social dialectic, slavery.

THE CASTLE

We are familiar with Duc de Blangis' well-known speech to his prisoners on the morning of the first of the "Hundred Twenty Days of Sodom": "You are shut up in an impregnable fortress. You are dead to the world and you draw breath only for our pleasure . . ." in that Chateau of Selliny which is explicitly mentioned at the end of *The Golden Age*. Sade's work is full of detailed descriptions of isolated strongholds (in savage and deserted countrysides, utterly cut off from the rest of the civilized world by an elaborate arrangement of impassable walls, dizzying precipices, and bridges which can be hurriedly blown up) that form the convent closed in by concentric walls, between which the victim's bodies rot away in the vertiginous lair of the ogre in "Juliette." In a corrupt and punctilious society, on the alert to correct aberrant desires, liberty makes these precautions necessary. A man alone, the sadist must jealously preserve that moral *independence* which he first had, reasonably, to impose on himself. To love as he wishes, completely, he must first enclose in parentheses all social constraints. He must *isolate* himself.

The confusion about sadism, resulting from a pernicious tradition, is such that one point must immediately be established. The castle has nothing in common, either in theory or in practice, with a concentration camp. However paradoxical it may seem, the "victims" are subjected to no constraint there, and Vadim's Nazi submachine guns are a misconception in a film otherwise rich in material. At the start, the chances are scrupulously equal. The strong must prove their power at every moment, and the weak will be so only because they constantly acquiesce to submitting themselves. If Justine is unhappy and Juliette happy, it is not that the one has had greater luck than the other, but because the first acquiesces and the second rejects — exploit or submit. Sadism is a shining victory over fate.

Also, from the point of view of this praiseworthy orthodoxy, the best illustration of the Sadean castle is that offered us in Ernest Beaumont Schoedsack and Irving Pichel's *The Most Dangerous Game*; for this, in spite of the rather spotty talents of the latter, capable of the best (*She*) but often poorly served by poor scripts for which he is, alas, largely responsible (*Destination Moon*), we must unhesitatingly give all the credit to the former.

On a stormy night, a ship misled by strange lights, is

wrecked on an unknown tropical island. The only survivor
is Bob Rainsford (Joel McCrea), big game hunter, face to
face with eternity. He succeeds in reaching the shore, and
through the storm makes his way, to a somber, medieval
castle at the high point of the island. At the portal, the door-
knocker is the figure of a centaur, wounded by an arrow and
carrying in his arms a woman with loose-flowing hair. A mute
and bestial servant who we will later learn is a Tartar (Noble
Johnson) greets the newcomer who finds two survivors of a
previous shipwreck in the great hall of the castle: Martin
Trowbridge (Robert Armstrong) and his sister, Eve (Fay
Wray). Then, gravely descending the great stone staircase,
stopping momentarily before a tapestry on which the figure of
the wounded centaur from the portal is repeated, comes, in
evening clothes and with an attentive politeness touched with
scarcely discernible irony, the lord of the manor, Count
Zaroff. He says he is enchanted by the arrival of Rainsford,
whose reputation is known to him. He himself is a great
hunter. He has tracked every game, down to the most dangerous, a buffalo that gave him the wound on the temple from
which he "still suffers" occasionally. But he was finally disillusioned by every kind of hunting until when, independent
on his island, he finally discovered the most noble hunt,
which, with his inimitable accent, he calls "the most dangerous
game" (Leslie Banks).

Rainsford and Eve soon discover the secret of the castle,
where mastiffs roam endlessly in a subterranean kennel, and
some hallways are decorated with sinister trophies, human
heads preserved in alcohol-filled jars. Confronted with Trowbridge's corpse, a clumsy and disappointing prey, they learn
that the Count's favorite sport is the hunt of man. To provide
himself with game he has installed a system of false beacons
to lure ships to their doom. The very difficulty of saving one-

self and reaching the craggy coast constitutes the first selection. Zaroff hunts only the choicest game, that which is worthy of him.

For he immediately dissipates doubts. His favorite game, although it is cruel, can only exist by perfect fairness. Zaroff gives the man he hunts maximum opportunity. He arms him with a knife and gives him a sufficient head-start. Finally, if at sunrise the fugitive is still alive he will have won his freedom. Such a thing has never really occurred but the prospect is actually the Count's secret dream. Thus, he declares: "The weak were put on earth to give pleasure to the strong. I am strong". He has only one desire, to find game worthy of him, as strong as he; in a word, to fight with equal weapons. This ideal game, he believes to have found, after many disappointments, in the hunter, Rainsford.

Rainsford accepts the stake and flees with Eve. A nightmarish chase begins through the misty swamps and forest, in a silence punctuated by the sound of flight, torn by the howling of the pack of hounds that Ivor, the servant, holds in leash. Zaroff springs one by one, the traps left by Rainsford, traps which, by the way, cost the Tartar his life. A few minutes before the time fixed for the end of the hunt, the dogs drive the young man to the edge of a cliff from which he throws himself. At last Zaroff can light one of his favorite cigarettes and pass on to the second act of his program: love. But upon entering the room where he should find Eve, he finds himself face to face with the man he thought he had vanquished, and who, in the course of the ensuing struggle, stabs him with one of his own arrows, used as a dagger.

Rainsford and Eve escape in a motor boat. As he hears the sound of the motor, in the most beautiful shot in the film, with a plastic severity which is not the least of its virtues,

Zaroff tries for the last time to draw his bow — and dies without succeeding.

Merian C. Cooper, the film's producer, declared "I don't think anyone among us knew Sade's work" (Michel Caen, in "Midi-Minuit Fantastique", No. 6, p. 41). One must therefore be content with that, and be satisfied with the notable and obligatory meeting of great minds. In *The Most Dangerous Game* and in the work of the Marquis we discover a similar choice given to the adversary — there is less irony than one might suppose in Zaroff's words, when, after having emphasized that he always gave his game a choice between passive death and the hunt, he affirms "Invariably, Mr. Rainsford, invariably they choose the hunt" — a similar offer of the possibility of morally raising oneself, in brief, the same concern. With a hundred and thirty years between them, Sade and Zaroff make an appeal, without weakness or indulgence, to the same rigidity of human nature.

The two remakes of *The Most Dangerous Game* — I mean those which claim to derive from Richard Connell's story, for Ted Tetzaff's *Johnny Allegro* is built around an obviously different story of far greater banality — are remarkable for a blunt insipidness which makes Schoedsack's genius all the more precious. Robert Wise, fortunately for him, was better inspired when he directed Edgar Barrier, who in comparison with Leslie Banks, is a popular dancer on the decline (*A Game of Death,* 1945). As for the chase in pallid Ray Boulting's *Run for the Sun* (1956), it is more like a glorified boy scout game than the devilish and unrestricted hunt in the *Game.* Both irrevocably sacrifice the moral fable for the sake of the criminal anecdote. Since the form suffers from the lack of a stark concept, it is not surprising that the glowering and sinister castles become, in their films, houses for nouveau riche gentlemen.

To find equivalent romanticism one must look elsewhere.

And first of all, it must be found as a place in which shock and horror are privileged. If the "House of Usher" falls once too often under the blows of Jean Epstein's glacial estheticism (*The Fall of the House of Usher,* 1928); many other dwellings, intangible inheritance from more than a century of gothic literature, have been very happily haunted. The same is true of vampire lairs. When once more on the other side of the bridge, among the somber hills, one sees the enormous portals of Nosferatu's castle slowly open of their own accord and discerns gliding smoothly from the shadows, the tall, thin silhouette of the lord of the manor. The geographic situation is just about immutable. In Nurnau's book, Utter comes to the foot of the Carpathians. In *Dracula,* Renfiel arrives one dark night at the little town of Bistritz in the heart of Central Europe. Count Mora, in *The Mark of the Vampire,* haunts Borotyn Castle near the village of Visoka, in Czechoslovakia. One reads in the synopsis of *The Daughter of Dracula;* "To those who believe in vampires, this strange and terrifying adventure of the Countess Marya Zaleska is dedicated. It is in Wirby, County Durham, in the moorlands, in the fogs and the wind, that it took place, then, later, in the deep gorges and stark countryside of Transylvania" ("Bizarre", No. 24-25, p. 66). Terence Fisher, scrupulously faithful, merely has to have Dracula cross a German border to regain his noble mountain dwelling, watched over by stone eagles (*Horrors of Dracula*).

One can therefore only deplore the blame-worthy fantasies, provoked by who knows what sort of taste for busywork alterations, that substituted for the "refuge forever closed to spying civilizations" (Alain Le Bris, "Midi-Minuit Fantastique", No. 1, p. 20), the factory of *Vampyr,* the sanatorium in *The Return of the Vampire* and, still worse, the museum of horrors in *House of Frankenstein.*

More modest in appearance than the castle, the haunted house displays definite and solid virtues. The home where objects mysteriously move by themselves belongs to the ABC of trick photography and is as old as the history of the movies; Harold Lloyd was thus rendering homage to a long tradition when he walked into one. Max Linder,, a comedian highly overrated by an imbecilic esthetic nationalism, found his best role a year before his death, when he entered the private hotel in Abel Gance's *Help!* (1924), where all the ghosts of Hell assaulted him in a well-orchestrated, geometric procession. The haunted house could then become the framework for two great horror classics.

The first of these undeniable masterpieces is James Whale's *Old Dark House* (1932). Benn Walter Levy had adapted J. B. Priestley's book with a freedom for which he may flatter himself. Lost, during a stormy night, on the moors of Wales, some travellers take refuge in an isolated dwelling that glows sinisterly by lightning flash. They spend a night of horror there. Every hallway, every dark corner, every cursed room is steeped in the terror of a dreadful secret. Broad daylight turns out to be even more frightening than the dark. The shadowy old house actually shelters a monster (played by Boris Karloff) who shows himself to be an extraordinary incarnation of a fury so elemental that it becomes almost abstract.

Twenty years later William Castle, a producer of so-called B films, as longwinded as he is uneven, was to surpass James Whale with his previously cited evocation, *The Night of All Mysteries.* Even the outside of the dwelling is resolutely demented, a sort of mad bunker where the cube seems to possess those restless and moving angles so common in Lovecraft's geometry. No one has spent the night there, and survived. The imprudent ones who take the risk, driven by the

desire for money, will, shepherded by Vincent Price at the
top of his form, pass, one by one, through the seven degrees
of abomination. The hanged swing in the hallways. The
coffers are full of decaying heads. The walls of the basement
open to let an old servant woman, transformed into a treacherous Errynie, emerge. Horror of horrors, even the outside,
the reassuring external world, seems wiped out and replaced
by a thick shadow that is ready to vomit the unspeakable: a
strangled corpse, or a rope, possessed with life, that winds
itself around a young girl's legs like a serpent. *The Night of
All Mysteries,* in spite of a rationalized ending, whose logic is
however happily deficient at more than one point, deserves
to rank as the classic of hallucinated claustrophobia.

The castle, as well as the house, may therefore be defined
as retreats, as isolated places where everything is possible,
above all the realization of so-called mad dreams. Entrenched
in a medieval castle an outlaw can rule the jungle (*Jungle
Jim*). The mad scientists install the machinery for their wild
inventions in their crypts. Not far from Baron Frankenstein's
dwelling, a half-ruined tower rises on a hilltop and here he
installs his laboratory. It is there that he patiently creates life,
reconstructing a man from fragments of corpses, that lightning,
in making the essential spark burst forth, animates. The settings of the first *Frankenstein* reach their high point in *Son
of Frankenstein* (Rowland V. Lee, 1939). Through the
windows of the train that takes him back to his father's castle,
Baron Wolf von Frankenstein can already see the countryside changing, becoming bare and misty. The castle itself,
with its interlaced pillars whose foundations are lost in the
shadow, and its twisted and dripping sculptures, and even the
neighboring village, are solid evidence of the expressionism
one must guard against rejecting as old-fashioned. This distortion does indeed show how it is possible to enter another

world, firmly free of banality, purged of the everyday and, consequently, eager to welcome all possibilities.

To perfect, unhampered, his personal experiments on life and, better still, on the essence of human nature, Doctor Moreau established his retreat on an unknown island in the Indian Ocean (Erle C. Kenton's *Island of Lost Souls*, 1932). There the jungle is peopled with furtive beings, humanoids created from animals by the doctor who subjects them to his rule and plays at master and slave with them. A dangerous game in which, he does not realize — this is the weakness from which he dies — that it is always possible to reverse the rules. The day that Moreau orders Gola, the ape-man, to kill a human being, he himself sets in motion the mechanism that will lead to his downfall. Convinced of the vulnerability of their gods by this example, the humanoids discover the possibility of revolt. They take Moreau prisoner, drag him to the "torture chamber" and submit him, in turn, to the vivisection of which they had been victims. The island does not survive the death of its master. It disappears, with its miserable creatures, who know only an instant of liberty, in a gigantic fire, before the eyes of the miraculously-escaped hero. An emulator of Moreau, Sir Joel Cadman, practices his blasphemous experiments in a secularized abbey whose cellars, as in *The Case of Charles Dexter Ward,* hold the abominable humanoids the scientist has created. Here, again, the prisoners break their chains and avenge themselves atrociously on their master (Reginald Le Borg's *The Black Sleep,* 1956).

Island for island, the West Indies yield nothing to the Indian Ocean where Welles' hero lived. They too have their own monsters, isolated from a frowning society, those corpses, animated through magical voodoo practice, called zombies. Michel Laclos writes on this subject: "By 1932 the movies discovered the living dead, those incredibly docile, walking corpses of which they were to make so much use. First it was *The Living Dead* by T. Hayes Hunter, followed in 1933 by Victor Halperin's *The Zombies.* Trusting some fragmentary but rather precise childhood memories, we described some sequences from *White Zombie,* the title then not known to us, as "Scenes from an Unknown Film" in No. 1 of "Bizarre" (First Series)."

The sequences in question were a flashing condensation of necrophilia and entombment. Laclos adds: "The scene takes place in a cemetery. Hiding behind a mausoleum, a man wrapped in a black cape spies, with a particularly joyful look, on the last phases of a burial . . .

"Later, in the middle of the night, while the rain and tempest rage, the man in black returns to the grounds; looks for a moment among the recent tombs; stops. Midnight strikes. The man pulls a delicately-worked wax figurine from his pocket; then, with sure movements, makes it melt above a flame *that never flickers once.* It is then that the door of a vault creaks open and that from its obscure depths, very beautiful and very pale there emerges — *the girl buried that afternoon.* She is clothed only in a shroud, or a long white robe which waves in the wind. Her loosed hair falls over her shoulders . . .

"In a street near the cemetery a closed carriage waits, and promptly bears away the man and the willing corpse . . .

"The castle of the man in black. Medieval architecture. Interminable corridors leading into immense and entirely empty rooms. The entire domestic staff is composed of these "living dead", snatched from the tomb on the evening of their burial. They are dumb, industrious and faithful.

"In one of the rooms of the castle there are secluded — for what dreadful purposes? — a young man and a young girl . . ." ("Esculape," June, 1960).

It is on an equally deserted island that Bela Lugosi tries and succeeds in creating zombies artificially. Finally, it is in an island castle that Dean Martin and Jerry Lewis blunder among the walking dead in *Scared Stiff* by George Marshall.

Not falling precisely into any of these traditions, five or six films, after *The Most Dangerous Game,* have carried the theme of the castle through different keys to its full flowering.

The Black Cat (1934), a better film, and quite unlike Edgar G. Ulmer's, has no strict relation to the novel by Edgar Allan Poe. Hermann Poelzig, from his own sketches, had a wild dwelling built on the summit of a mountain loaded with dynamite. The action takes place, it must be specified, in the Carpathians. Great adept of black magic, Poelzig in this palace "strange as life and death" leads an existence of logical desire, playing chess with the woman he loves, and regarding with nostalgia his old mistresses in their cataleptic state, walled in niches behind crystal casings. He, claiming a cat's nine lives, is killed by the Enemy of the Cats himself, by that which cannot see a black cat without slaying it, and, most shockingly, skinning it alive.

In regard to the theme of the castle, the year 1935 proved truly remarkably rich. There was on the one hand, *The Raven* by Louis Friedlander; the scenario, signed David Boehm, being an erudite tribute to Edgar Allan Poe. We have already spoken of the torture apparatus knowledgeably conceived by Dr. Vallin but it is necessary to dwell once more on the cogently organized artifice of the decor, of seeping tunnels and sinister and shadowy rooms which are such a challenge to the normal. On the other hand, there was the *Black Room* by Roy William Neill, which transposed to Central Europe Gilles de Ray's defiances. A medieval lord, lying in wait in his towers for the terrified peasants whose daughters he makes mysteriously disappear, Boris Karloff dares to defy even

Fate itself before his corpse, pierced with a dagger, is preci-
pitated into the subterreanean charnel-house where he had
disposed of the tortured bodies of his victims.

In 1952, it was Austria's turn to be peopled with the
sadistic manor lords of the cinema. *The Black Castle* by
Nathan Juran brings us back to the very end of the eighteenth
century. Count Von Bruno (Stephen MacNally) who fills the
moats of his castle with crocodiles, and who looses a black
panther to stalk through the fog in pursuit of the unfaithful
wife and her lover, is not worthy of Count Zaroff, his moral
ancestor.

In *The Blood of the Vampire* (Henry Cass, 1958), a young
doctor, unjustly condemned for devoting himself to experiments in blood transfusion, is shut in a fortress for insane
criminals that is isolated on the moors and surrounded by
double walls between which ravenous mastiffs tirelessly prowl.
The warden of this prison indulges, with complete freedom,
in the most daring biological experiments, for which he prefers
to use, rather than guinea pigs, young and pretty women.

But the most perfect example of the contemporary Sadean
castle should probably be sought somewhere else; where, at
first, one would never dream of finding it. However, the palace
in *Last Year at Marienbad* (Alain Resnais, 1961) corre-
sponds, quite precisely, to that which one has a right to expect in these secret dwellings. The non-Euclidean geometry
of the corridors (apparently straight-lines, but in which one
nevertheless gets lost) and its park (laid out in mysterious
crossroads of time, and where everything seems possible),
correspond admirably to the isolated, closed, jealously double-
locked, universes which Sade took pleasure in describing in
detail throughout his books. Its severe layout, all the greater
in borrowing nothing from classic architecture, is like the
very reflection of a moral severity. The confrontations which

occur in the palace actually have, spiritually, nothing to envy those in (Juliette). The game of Nim, while less spectacular than the whip, rape, or the knife, is, in the hands of Sacha Pitoeff who could lose if he liked, but doesn't want to, no less a perfectly subtle and effective instrument of domination. The ardent romanticism, completely inspired by the goddess films of 1910 and thereabouts, by its very character of madness and empty explosion, finally could be pleasing only to those of whom, Gilbert Lely has said, the whole thing "is love."

BONDAGE

Let us for the last time make one thing clear. Bondage, enslavement considered only as such, like the desire to humiliate, has no place in Sade. Nor has the converse pleasure. If it happens that the heroes have themselves flogged, or tied up, this is never from a taste for passivity, but for erotic purposes exactly as when they take the active part. The girl victim should never consent, far less derive pleasure. Her resistance is not merely added spice; it is an absolutely necessary condition without which the very dominance of the torturer would be debased. If it is true that, clinically, sadism and masochism oppose and complement each other, the morality of Sade and of Sacher-Masoch are nonetheless fundamentally irreconcilable. The passion for freedom is not compatible with the joy of being a slave, nor with the taste for submissiveness. Let us reiterate: Justine, on the one hand, is fully responsible for her wretched destiny, and on the other hand she finds no pleasure in her misfortunes.

This granted, it is still true that the semantic requirements of popularization must be taken into account. The bondage that hardly has meaning or place on the level of Sadean morality shows up everywhere at the level of algomania. In films, it makes such good box office that distributors drag in, with obvious ecstasy, the word "slave" whenever they can; sometimes when scarcely appropriate. This is how the mediocre *Tragedy of Rigeletto* by Flavio Calzavera, inspired by Victor Hugo and Verdi, saw itself rechristened *The King's Slave,* though the wretched baffoon really did not deserve that title.

All cinematic bondage is, in the first place, force exercised on women. Films set in antiquity, or the biblical or early Christian periods are rich in captives subjected to every humiliation and every torment. We have already cited, for other purposes, DeMille's films and various historic works both old and new, *The Slaves of Carthage* in particular but others as well. The Gauls who attack Rome in Sergio Grieco's *Roman Slave* have in their ranks a young and handsome warrior. Captured by the Romans, this warrior turns out to be a woman, Rossanna Podesta, who is not particularly grieved at being subjected to a conqueror. Isabelle Corey, persecuted Christian, in Mario Bonnard's *Slave of the Orient,* finds herself cast into prison, where she becomes dear friends with one of her sisters-in-misery, Irene Tunc. Both become slaves of the queen and, after Isabelle barely escapes being burned alive, everything ends happily.

Another region blessed by slavery is the southern United States. Once we have mercifully sidestepped the slaveholding or Uncle-Tomish inspiration originating with Griffith, we must speak of Raoul Walsh's admirable *Band of Angels* (1952). This film, the most accurate and many-sided in dealing with racism, tells the story of a quadroon girl, Yvonne DeCarlo, whose Negro blood (despite her white skin) delivers her into the hands of a "humane" master: Clark Gable. We witness, during the Civil War, through violence and hypocrisy, Gable's pangs of conscience, his discussions with Sidney Poitier, educated slave whose discourse would not be rejected by the Fanon in *Damned of the Earth*. The end is as satisfying as could be desired. The white and the black confront each other, man to man, having equal need of each other; brothers, therefore, and as proud of being men as the protagonists of Bunuel's *The Young One* that has more than one point in common with Walsh's film.

Although they constitute the majority, the women do not quite have exclusive rights to the privilege of erotic bondage. Men can be captured by vigorous warriors; like Don Taylor in Curt Siodmak's *Love Slaves of the Amazon* (1954) (at least the title is startling), who finds himself a prisoner of a legendary race of women in Brazil, who are forced to capture the men needed for the continuation of their kind. By an entirely natural logic, the captive men of *The Queen of the Amazons* (again an ancient race), reduced to domestic tasks — cooking, sewing and laundry — feminize themselves in an outrageous fashion. The masculine voluptuousness of humiliation (which in the very beautiful *Salome* visually inspired by Beardsley's studied and marvelously depraved calligraphy, manifests itself in the scene of a robust slave kneeling before the delicate and imperious Nazimova) culminates in weird situations. The noble Lex Barker, descendant of an ancient patrician family of Louisiana, to gain a postponement from his creditor, is reduced to selling himself into slavery to him, but later to her, for it involves Patricia Medina, a white-trash whorehouse madam. In satisfying her hatred of aristocrats, Patricia spares the magnificent Lex no humiliation (*Duel on the Mississippi*, William Castle). Let us finally cite the short Japanese film, of which Alain Joubert says, in "Presence du Cinema" (Nos. 6-7, p. 40): "A few short subjects, like *A Day in the Life of a Queen*, initiate us into the behavior of Nipponese masochists. The lover of humiliations should arouse his mistress by licking the soles of her feet, which will put her into a charming humor with him. He will serve as her dressing-table during her ablutions, and will be severely flogged if he overturns the glass containing her false teeth, which she has placed upon his back, and he will finish by executing all his idol's caprices, much as the best-trained trick dogs would do."

Prisoners are always sisters to slaves. *The Mouse Cage,* by Jean Gourguet, with Dany Carell as the lead, contains practically nothing but heroic inmates, who rescue a handsome aviator from the claws of the Gestapo, and who are luckier than those in World War I, including an American girl who, like Marie Walcamp, was imprisoned in a cave full of skeletons (Henry McRae's *Liberty, A Daughter of the U. S. A.,* 1916). *The Snake Pit* by Anatole Litvak, houses the incurably insane; and Olivia de Havilland recovers her reason there, through the very excess of horror. *The Angels of Sin* (1943), by Robert Bresson, are religious members of one of those convents where, as everyone knows since Diderot's "The Nun", amusing things can happen; those voluptuous kisses on the foot, for example, that are such a joy to Bunuel. But he is also involved with far more classical prisons.

Prisons Without Bars, shown before the war, and afterwards *Women's Prison* by Maurice Cloche (1958), represent the zero point of the genre. Danielle Darrieux, then Danielle Delorme, struggled between rehabilitating education and the injustice of a judicial blunder. *Caged,* by the talented and little-known John Cromwell, has an entirely different interest. There, Eleanor Parker degenerated little by little, in contact with criminal women, and endured ill-treatment by a barbarous warden (Agnes Moorehead) who, among other wickednesses, punishes her by shaving her head. The end of *Caged* is resolutely and correctly pessimistic. In it Cromwell declares the total futility of the penal system. The freed convict, after having, as the saying goes, paid her debt, sooner or later will have to return to prison. Alain Joubert, in the article cited, speaks of the Japanese *"Among the Convicts,* the life of a woman thief, slightly out of her mind, who does a strip-tease act in her cell to entertain and gratify some of her companions."

It happens, though rarely it is true, that imprisonment occurs for clearly erotic purposes. These captivities, which can be determinedly degrading, like for the women delivered to the SS in Hermann Millakowsky's *Women in Bondage,* can also be marvelously poetic. Through a window of the mad gambling house run by Mother Gin Sling, bamboo cages are seen being lowered — to the strains of a Schubert melody — that contain half-naked girls (Joseph Von Sternberg's *Shanghai Gesture,* 1942).

The prisons themselves are of various kinds. There is the medieval tower of *Prisoner of the Tower of Fire* of G-W Chili, where Milly Vitale is held captive by Elisa Cegani (1952). There is the idealized Moorish palace where, to change the postulates of the problem slightly, it is a young officer of the British Navy, Donald Sinden, whose jailers are charming girls in transparent undress (*You Know What Sailors Are,* Ken Annakin, 1954). There is also, and above all, the floating prison *Ship of Lost Women* by Raffaelle Matarazzo, where the atmosphere of erotic madness and flagellation reaches its climax in a terrifying hurricane of fire and blood, admirably photographed by the great Aldo Tonti. Led by Kerima, the unchained prisoners offer themselves to the sailors who have been ordered to suppress their revolt. Maritime adventures are, moreover, rich in beautiful captive girls. Let us call to mind *Conquerors of a New World* by Cecil B. DeMille, and his prisoners destined to establish homes in the (surely) virgin lands of North America; and let us underline the relative importance of recent pirate films by Domenico Paolella. Here we cite the *Secret of the Black Hawk* (1961), where Lex Barker rescues Nadia Marlova from the slaughter that rages through a Caribbean island; and the *Terror of the Seas* (1961), where Chance Island, a buccaneer's hide-out, is populated by ravishing, captive girls ruled by Sylvana Pampanini, or even, most recently, *Island of Lost Women,* where Federica Ranchi and Michele Mercier, deported to Devil's Island, are freed by chivalrous pirates. All these films prove through true skill and excellent judgment, floggings and rapes the erotic attraction of imprisonment and submission. Of a kindred inspiration, let us finally cite *Westward The Women,* by William Wellman (1951). Eager to find women for the men of his ranch, Robert Taylor recruited volunteers and, like a cattle-drive to Abilene, forced them to cross the desert, under his strict supervision. But bit by bit, reacting to Denise Darcell, he stops being a woman-hater.

From the treatment of slaves to the treatment of white-slaves is only a very short step. The filmography of the subject, under the pretext (more or less hypocritical) of denouncing it, is (rather more than less) interminable; so I must limit myself to a few recent examples. The subject, really supremely international, seems to enjoy particular favor in West Germany. In *Mannequins for Rio,* by Kurt Neumann (1954), five models come to Rio seeking work. The garment house operated by Gisela Fackeldey is, as they quickly find out, a bordello, and every attempt to escape is severely punished, as Ingrid Stenn painfully learns. In Holland the pimps of Maria Rabenalt's *Call Girls* (1957) provide young flesh, and Ingmar Zeisberg is the prey of Erwin Strahl. *Girl Street,* by Hermann Kugelstadt (1960) is a typical Hamburg melodrama. The film about prostitution is, however, only one avatar of the black film. *Silver Moon Cafe,* by Wolfgang Gluck, portrays a gang of jewel thieves, and depicts the imprisonment of Marisa Nell by Marina Petrova in the "Silver Moon" cabaret. Likewise *Girls for the Mambo-Bar,* by the same specialist, Gluck, scrambles together prostitution, drug traffic and Communist spying.

France is not backward, Agnes Laurent, white slaver in *Girl Market* by Maurice Cloche, is confronted by the classic charming situation in South America. Leo Joannon has, on this theme, made one of those burlesque and ferociously anti-clerical films of which he has the knack. Trabaud, working priest at Montmarte, is rescued by the big-hearted whore, Annie Giraudot. Killed by gangsters to whom she has refused to reveal the priest's hiding-place, she dies in the ambulance which takes her through a swarm of kids receiving first communion, while she murmurs "Everything is white . . ." Eduoard Molinaro demonstrates this more seriously. *Missing Women* depicts a sinister villa where Magali Noel seduces innocent young girls, helped by Estella Blain, with whips and drugs, for the sexual appetites of gangsters. The co-plot finally becomes the theme. Lucianno Emmer directs Marina Vlady in *The Girl in the Glass Cage,* whose sufficiently dismal action takes place at Anvers.

Japan has not escaped this "social plague". The American occupation has made little tea-houses prosper and geishas multiply. *Soldiers' Girls* (1957), by Kiyoski Komoni, recounts the long, sad and melodramatic calvary of one of these, Fumika; all things — drugs, blows, tragic deaths of successive fiances — combine for the surer degradation of the wretched woman. Alain Joubert, again, says: "Along with the *social-psychological* films, the sketches are equally numerous. One singles out particularly the stories of bad youths forcing poor girls, fresh from far-off battlefields, to prostitute and to drug themselves under threats of many (unspecified) tortures.

Sooner or later they become restless (perhaps from retro-
spective disgust, perhaps from remorse, as suits the scriptwriter) and the threats finally become concrete, for the greater
pleasure of the viewer. *Okinu Otama* presents, as a climax,
the torture of a recalcitrant prostitute, chained naked, head
down, with burning wax pouring between her breasts. The
torture chamber holds the spotlight in these films which would
not exist without them." (Op. cit., pp. 38-39.)

The United States is much more discreet and allusive. The
bordello is one of the traditional settings in the Western, one
of the institutions of the decadent South. The weird *Walk on
the Wild Side* (1961) by Edward Dmytryck unreels itself
during the "Roaring 20's" in New Orleans. Capucine is a
lodger of the lesbian Barbara Stanwyck who, married to a
legless cripple, develops for her lodger a passion that leads
to her death.

The situation of modern servants is sometimes not so very
different from the fate of slaves. It is possible, in the tradition
of the precious slavey, to create scenes of charming and delicate amusement, as in *Lisbon* (1956) by Ray Milland, in
which Claude Raines surrounds himself with a harem of
ravishing starlets in lacy aprons and white gloves; he spoils
them paternally, and, to punish them, occasionally burns the
dresses he had offered them. This situation, in reverse, with
Jerry Lewis in *The Ladies' Man* (1960), directed by himself
is — despite the burlesque situation — appreciably more disturbing. As the only bellboy in a hotel for single ladies run by
a regal directress, spoon-fed like a newborn babe, his adventures present, at moments, the nightmarish side of various
masochistic novels. The interaction of Ulf Palme and Anita
Bjork, in *Mlle. Julie* (1954) by Alf Sjoberg, a love affair
between valet and mistress, in recalling troubled memories of
childhood and of foot-fetichism, when heightened to baroque

delirium, expresses far more clearly the taste of brooded over humiliation and domination. More perplexing as to the naivete of the authors, is *A Husband on a Leash,* by Henri Levin (1963), where Micheline Presle persuades Sandra Dee to treat her husband, Bobby Darin, exactly and literally like a dog; he comes to enjoy this so much that at the end of the film he crouches in a kennel, a studded dog collar around his neck. Finally, the drama explodes, and household slaves raise the flag of revolt, in the hysterical film by Nico Papatakis (1963). Michel Flacon tells us: "Inspired, like *The Maids,* by the affair of the Papin sisters, *The Depths* seems to offer us the ingredients of the heaviest rural realism: idiots from Bordeaux, a decayed land, money quarrels, the last disasters of an 'honorable' family at the end of the road. Embarked on this vessel, two young servant-girls, unpaid, starved and exploited, in mounting rage pushed their revolt against their employer as far as an orgy of grandiose and heady violence. They become, with plentiful curses and many blows, sabotaged cooking and artful traps, witches in a state of acute hysteria, damned women, intoxicated avengers. The film is the vociferous and tumultuous chronicle of this organized pillage, of this psychosis of depravity and destruction, the only outcome open to them." ("Cinema 63," n. 7, p. 33.)

The state of helplessness brought about by being chained, is not the least attraction of slavery. Beautiful captive girls and robust chained men, like *Tarzan and the Leopard Woman* (Kurt Neumann, 1946), populate the serials, old films and Westerns such as Delmer Daves' *The Last Wagon,* where Richard Widmark, hands tied, is dragged along the ground, Eastern fiction, with Noelle Adam imprisoned by Fausto Tossi and tied up in the *Arabian Nights* (by Henri Levin and Mario Bava), or finally, the hell of *Maciste* and of *Hellzapoppin.* Curious love scenes are then possible, the partners linked by manacles (*The 39 Steps* and *Fifth Column* by Alfred Hitch-cock), or even completely tied up, as in *I, the Jury* by Harry Essex, where Margaret Sheridan crawls on the ground in order, despite her bonds, to come closer to Biff Elliot, fastened to a chair under a spotlight. Let us quote one last time the penerating article by Joubert: "The consequences of war and marital jealousy wed curiously in *Imashine (Game of Words)*. Here is the melodramatic scenario. On returning to Japan after the Sino-Japanese war, the hero is told by a doctor that he will not be able to father a child because of venereal diseases contacted during his journeys. Time passes. One day he learns that his wife is pregnant by a young student. The remembrance of pleasure which he once took in torturing Chinese prisoners stimulates him to efforts of the same kind. He therefore ties up his wife for a whole night, in an extremely uncomfortable position, exposed to the gaze of passersby. The next morning, overjoyed at having indulged his sadistic urges, he confides in a friend who advises him to repeat the experience regularly. This he hastens to do, with touching faithfulness. The least pretext is enough for him to tie the culprit, first to the ground, then to the electric cables of his workshop, where she ends by meeting death by electrocution." (Op. cit., pp. 39-40.)

The erotic relationships themselves often develop under the contrasting signs of master and slave, when such classi-fication is a priori possible. Robert Henayoun, in his cited article ("Presence du Cinema" no. 6-7, pp. 11-12), writes: "Certain actors' temperaments in the sparse episodes of 'black' production are especially apt, let us say, to evoke the genius of sadism: these occur in actors as different (apart from their physique) as George MacReady, Paul Henreid, Lee Marvin, Raymond Burr, or Stephen MacNally, whom directors never fail to set homosexually against accomplished masochists like

Burt Lancaster or Alan Ladd. Just as the masculine sadistic
attributes are discerned (by careful study) as coolness, precise
actions, irresistible initiative, and icy humor, so one finds them
in the fair sex in ambiguity and slow movements, the exasper-
ating gift of evasion, and the contemptuous trick of non-
accepting. Marlene Dietrich, Ona Munson, Anita Bjork, and
the old Rita Hayworth have projected all the seduction of
dedicated mentors in *Blue Angel, The Woman and the Puppet,
Shanghai Gesture, Mlle. Julie,* or *The Lady from Shanghai.*
In the third film, Mother Gin Sling, a feminine version of
Blangis, officiates like a priestess at the catalog of forbidden
orgies. In Von Sternberg's masterpiece, the sadistic ritual
attains a perfection which is made unbearable by etiquette and
costume, the perfect baroque decor, the effect of imprisonment, and the spectacular promiscuity of abjectness.

Slavery, finally, is a personal affair, not only for junkies
(*The Slave,* by Ciampi, 1954) and drunkards (*The Lost
Weekend,* by Billy Wilder, 1946), in their skillfully faked
torments, but for Torre Nilsson's heroines secluded in their
patrician homes; the Elsa Daniel of *Angel's House* (1957)
and of *The Hand in the Trap* (1961) is equally a prisoner of
circumstances, of suffocating social and religious constraints,
which end by stifling her half-formed wishes of revolt. Luis
Bunuel, in *The Destroying Angel* (1961) (a film of infinite
richness of which this is only one aspect) describes moral and
intellectual prisons, constructed by the prisoner's own hands
— the bourgeois salons and churches.

GENRES AND CREATORS

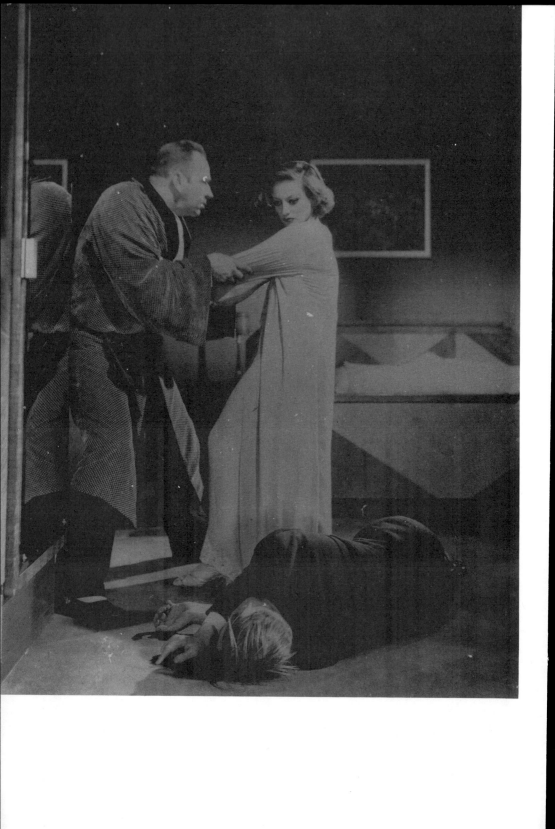

Having dealt with the commonest of the areas most difficult to investigate, the accidental or the allusive, the fact remains that in the cinema sadism shows through in some genres and the work of certain directors with an insistence that must be considered.

Whether this is voluntary or involuntary is not a crucial question. In fact, there has never been but a single filmmaker whose relationship with Sade has been established, on the conscious level, as that of an equal: Luis Bunuel.

CHARLIE CHAPLIN

Charlie Chaplin's career, based on regarding him as *the* incontestable genius (which one has no *right* to doubt) of film history, some critics have transformed into an enigma. One watches him go from absolute cruelty — trampling on dogs and children, beating up cripples, cheating, and even wheedling a pederast with the most disgusting blubbering — to becoming a collector of abandoned waifs, a protector of young blind people or even a tender lover numbed by neurasthenic dancers; in short, from common sadism to vulgar

163

masochism. What Agee acclaimed should astonish nobody. It is enough to read: "But when in the ordinary man, maso-chism remains a pathological state, the creative artist can purify it, can transfigure it into an act of redemptive morti-fication; the comedian becomes, from then on, the scapegoat of universal suffering as Jean Duvignaud most appropriately said in his study of 'the Chaplin Myth' ", or again: "One must admire the outspokenness of Chaplin, telling us the whole intimate tragedy of one who — after having made the whole world laugh — becomes aware of the futile and totally ridicu-lous character that must finally be abandoned to enter old age with simple and noble grandeur" to see basic orthodoxy get its ears boxed. Wretched as these remarks may be, they are still disquieting, and one must hold Chaplin at least partially responsible.

Certainly there is a dialectic, a necessary sliding from black to white and from plus to minus. But one will admit that that dialectic is closer to morbid confusion than to anything else, and above all, is not social criticism. Georges Sadoul would certainly be interested in giving up a little of his smug admira-tion, to reread — or read — what Aleksander Lejtes: ("Chaplin") had said in 1920 — "Knowledge of the nature of man is at the very basis of every success." Chaplin explained his own artistic success through his knowledge of human na-ture. But how can one understand human nature if one separates the human quality from society and social conflict? "The essence of man is not an abstract principle inherent in the isolated individual. In reality, it is a complex of social relationships," Marx said. There is neither transfiguration (let us not nail Chaplin to the Christian cross) nor trans-formation — at the very most, misgivings, even remorse, at the pathological level. It is thus necessary to make the dicho-tomy of Raymond Borde's article in "Positif", and hold in contempt the sniveling and compassionate Chaplin as much as one passionately admires the cruel Chaplin.

Chaplinesque cruelty has, indeed, its principal strength in being absolute. It respects absolutely nothing. It is sometimes the revenge of the weak upon the strong — blowing up of institutions (*Shoulder Arms, The Pilgrim, Easy Street, Monsieur Verdoux*) — but also simple assertion of pure wickedness (*The Champion, A Woman* or *The Pawnshop*). One imagines that the little consideration Charlie has for his brothers in misery, whose stinks disgust him when he sees himself forced to go to bed in a flop-house, the savage way he battles other unemployed men, as well as the purely accidental character of his social protests — it is by chance, having picked up a red rag fallen from a truck, that he finds himself at the head of a demonstration — are shocking to a Soviet critic, just as the end of *A Dog's Life* (where a litter of puppies replaces the baby in the crib which a young couple affectionately contemplates) will perhaps at another point similarly be shocking. But it remains true that this absolute mockery has an indisputable tonic value.

Everything happens this way and as Borde has likewise strongly pointed out, there is a long and progressive decline. The load of sadism, which is at its highest in the Keystone, Essenay, and Mutual films, begins to lessen in First National, with the tear-jerker sweetness of *The Kid*. Love itself, which made *In The Park* a frenetic manifesto, later was watered down, in unobjectionable taste, to cloying sentimentality. After the nadir of flabbiness in *Limelight* the downgrade becomes too hard to climb again and, despite the frequent excellence of its intentions, *A King in New York* (1957) only with difficulty, and only in rare flashes, rises above the level of the adventures of lovable uncle.

Though one must be on guard against all systematization

and remember that the Chaplinesque personality is — in a way — not reducible to influences, it is no less necessary to consider attentively the remarkable live sources of this later deterioration. It may be asked what Chaplin might have been without Mack Sennett.

Doubtless the most prodigious American producer, he brought to focus, during the eight years of his apogee (1912-20), the machinery of a permanent upheaval. In the madness of driverless cars, through fires, explosions, plunges off cliffs, downgrades, and falls from windows infinitely multiplied, in the hurricane of custard-pies and tidal waves of molasses, between runaway locomotives and outrageous cops, a dozen heroes, from Fatty Arbuckle to Al St. John, and from Ben Turpin to Chester Conklin, served (their unsinkable gaze riveted on the lovely lines of bathing beauties) as the devoted instruments of total destruction. The best of them, apart from Chaplin, went on to fashion this inexhaustible, but often uncontrolled and wild energy, to the style of their individual personalities. Harold Lloyd, the least gifted, nevertheless managed to transform the average man's stubbornness into an almost likable quality; which he raised at least once, in climbing a skyscraper wall, into pure vertigo. Harry Langdon asserted the perpetual victory of dream over reality. Buster Keaton became the tightrope walker of the impossible. And finally, W. C. Fields, made himself the magnificently eloquent apostle of sarcasm.

Stan Laurel and Oliver Hardy, before sinking into the quicksand of conventionality and losing their way among comic songs, were a team rich in double-meaning and in hidden powers methodically set free. The relationship between the fat effeminate, confident and brutal, and the little whiner, subject to sudden rages, is actually not really unusual, but the advantage lies in the strictly unpredictable consequences

of this unnatural union. There was a time when, where Laurel
and Hardy had gone, grass would not grow again. Because
of their influence, kicks in the shin attained the level of
social plague; creampuff battles between truckloads of participants becomes Dantesque. Arguments among drivers end by
demolishing the vehicles; and a quarrel with a landlord by
cold-blooded destruction of his property. Homes exploded to
the rhythm of gas-stoves. The old well on an isolated farm,
filled with alcohol by racketeers, waits patiently for someone
to draw its 'water' to put out a fire. Bulbs in neon-signs
change into feed-belts for machineguns. Burnt, crushed, their
feet planted in tubs of concrete, their fingers transformed into
matches, buried under sand, threatened with dissection, Laurel
and Hardy for 20 years knew how to juggle with their misfortunes, as well as with their dogged revenge on any random
victim.

The violence of the Marx brothers is of a very different kind.
It consists, in equal proportions, of purely verbal insolence
by Groucho (expert in maddening feints and gay deceits)
and of the primordial appetites of Harpo, for whom the
sight of every pretty girl released a chain-reaction of declarations in form of bites, and of tender outpourings based on
breaking her limbs. The logic of the fast-talker, and the urges
rooted in the mute's unpredictableness — the other brothers
occasionally lending hand or voice to one or the other — re-
sulted in a disintegration of the world and of life, suddenly
deprived of the laws of logic and physics.

Before finishing with slapstick, it is appropriate to cite a
series of short films (1945-55) created for MGM, with some
charm, by Pete Smith. The hero had a quality of attracting
catastrophes the way a magnet attracts iron filings. The most
innocent household object, under his expert fingers, was converted into an infernal machine. This transformation was

always in the service of an extraordinary cruelty. A finger glued to the burning surface of an electric oven, freed only with the help of an egg-turner, treacherous hammocks, boomerangs possessed of malignant life, and wildly rolling plates are there only to provoke, in the most straightforward way, emotions that are the more violent because these devices never stray from the most familiar. The rules of the game develop, and the films take on the aspect of quizzes, which MGM was producing in quantity at this time. He will fall, that is for sure, but will he fall here, there or there? This series marked the intrusion of the Do-It-Yourself into the sadistic territory.

It seems, moreover, that the good Louis B. Mayer secretly — perhaps unconsciously — had created, within his respectable establishment, secluded chambers where strange, and surely abnormal designs, were being woven. This was the cartoon corner.

In the matter of sexual cruelties — aside from some witches deliberately created to terrify little kids who knew how to survive them — one can remember in Disney only his curious affection for babies' bottoms; he has managed to introduce in, say, the most incongruous fashion (like the animated clock in *Pinocchio*), spankings of little children into his various films.

William Hannah and Joe Barbera were of a different kidney. The merciless war in which they involved Tom and Jerry, with the occasional help of cats from various gutters, of the bulldog Bop and his son Be-Bop, plus some cannibals and termites, systematically called on all the resources of squashing, exploding, or burning. To amuse his little girl friend, Tom makes Jerry into a yo-yo, or makes him dance on a saucer which he heats with charcoal. Thrown bricks produce gaps in a row of teeth. Teeth can also be smashed before crumbling into powder. Tom, falling from a plane into the ocean, breaks into a multitude of little fragments which slowly sink. The cat's whiskers are torn from him, one by one, by a guitarist needing strings for his instrument. Finally, bodies are molded into astonishing shapes: heads melt into the frying pan which clunks them; bodies are crushed into paw-shaped pancakes, or checkered in the image of the ventilator grille against which they have been pressed. Finally, a match, and flesh and bones are consumed in a lightning flash, leaving the victim nothing but a silhouette of ashes.

At a far higher level, Tex Avery plays more happily on systematic madness than on cruelty. The Mad Squirrel or Chilly Willy exercise only moral compulsions, but with such persistence that they achieve brainwashing, pure and simple. But pure cruelty is never absent, and in at least two films, it is found heightened to a quasi-metaphysical level. Fleeing from men, the misanthropic tomcat of *The Cat Who Hated People* takes refuge on the moon and is pursued by terrifying monsters, all jaws, or all pincers; and especially by a pencil-sharpener armed with paws, which captures him and neatly sharpens the tip of his tail. *Bad Luck Blackie* pushes the resources of plasticity to their climax. The huge dog, cruel and sneering, literally flows the length of the wall and corners his victim, the little white cat; on a shelf, he transforms him into a book all ready to be paged through — its title is "Kitty Foyle"; the black cat, badluck-carrier, in order to cross the path of the brute and to cause bad luck to fall upon him, in the shower of objects that range from bricks to battleships, lengthens himself, inflates himself, makes himself thin, or worms his way, with surprising ease. The actual ending of the film is astonishing. Having transformed himself, with aid of a paint-pot, into a jinx, the innocent and pretty white cat begins — in the final shot — to sneer diabolically.

At Warner Brothers, the spirit of the modern cartoon,

contemptuous as it should be of merely graphic audacity, reached its highest inspiration with Sylvester the cat and Tweetie-Pie the canary who are locked in a combat as fierce as and more exemplary than that which involves Tom and Jerry. Tweetie's sole weapon is an astonished innocence ("I tawt I taw a Puddy Tat"), which sets itself beyond even hypocrisy. Under his candid glance, Sylvester sees his gastro-nomic projects end in terror. Let him try to cross, by the most ingenious means, a garden covered by a veritable sea of ferocious dogs, into which he must fall if nobody helps him, and we clearly hear his bones crunching in their jaws. Dog, cat and canary, by dint of pursuing each other freneti-cally among automobiles, find themselves hospitalized (*Greedy for Tweetie*), each with limbs in splints, whose painful mem-bers become the objects of the most atrocious outrages; a hammer-blow is only an appetizer, and dynamite the common-est ingredient. How astonishing then, at the very end of this madness, to see Tweetie made big and ferocious by Dr. Jekyll's brew, *eating the cat*.

"This being granted," writes Robert Benayoun in *"Presence du Cinema,"* nos. 6-7, p. 55, "it is quite obvious that the animated cartoon is not, *cannot* be, truly sadistic. Far from exalting cruelty, it lessens and annihilates it in its sequences and its effects. Pain lives there only as a figment, like those in drunken dreams. Total burning or explosion transforms the victim into a temporary version of Uncle Tom. Teeth just broken grow back almost immediately in a smile all the more sardonic. The body, just cracked and smashed like fragile pottery, quickly regains its elasticity.

Accurate at first glance, the remark, on reflection, requires some qualification. Invulnerability, if it robs suffering of its immediate seriousness, by depriving death or mutilation of their horror, appears to add, on the other hand, to their deeper powers. As in those tortures where death is withheld because it would be a deliverance, the cartoon does not lessen the intensity of physical suffering. If the coyote, in pursuit of the road-runner were killed, as should happen on falling from the height of a precipice (*Scrambled Aches, Zoom and Bored, Hot Rod and Reel,* etc.), it would have, to its own mitigation and our disappointment, ended this exhausting hunt through a wildly inhuman country. The most terrifying thing about Hell is its eternity.

This principle is demonstrated in a quasi-mathematical fashion by Charles M. "Chuck" Jones, author of the cited road-runner and of the most inspired series from the very gifted Warner lot. Ralph, the coyote, and Sam, the shepherd dog, get up every morning before dawn to do their daily work which, the opposite of Count Zaroff's hunt, lasts from sunrise to sunset. They arrive at the edge of a valley where sheep graze, to punch timecards, like good workers, and take their places, Sam, the guard, at the edge of the cliff, and Ralph, the hunter, at the bottom, among the sheep. The sun rises; the siren howls; and the game begins (*Steal Wolf, Double or Mutton*). Its rules are classical: Ralph must catch a sheep, and for that he utilizes the most ingenious plans; but he always finds the immovable and impassive Sam blocking his path; and the subtle devices which he has created turn against him to crush him. Thus, delimited in time and space, constrained by the basic rules of civilized life, walled up within the very mechanism of the situation, the cartoon skims over an infinity of freaks and giddinesses. At the very end of the last I've seen in this series, *A Sheep In The Deep,* where the workday has been cut even shorter by a lunch-hour, Ralph is, at this point, so beat, that on the road back, Sam says, like a good buddy: "Don't knock yourself out. Rest tomorrow. I'll work for the both of us."

Remote from this pure aggression, some directors, surely unconsciously, with a success equal, more or less, to their intentions, have attempted to become the filmers of cruelty. Four or five of them, and one who firmly puts himself apart and alone, Bunuel, should, at least briefly, be discussed.

There was a time — 1945-50 — when, from the church of St. Germain des Pres to the Place Maubert, the name of Erich von Stroheim bore the dignity of a household word. This vilified filmmaker, whose character was too forceful, and soul too proud and too generous to have come to terms with Hollywood, this haughty authority, stern moralist (because he observed, without illusion, the teeming human vilenesses), the author of *Queen Kelly* saw forming around his head a halo of pride, cruelty and derision. To look at him a little more attentively, the reality is different enough. This tolerance of ugliness and sordidness, this preference for weakness and mockery, united with an amazed fascination at the most trivial fairy tale and the worst melodrama, hardly exceed the bounds of puritan stupidity. To dream that one is really wicked because one dwells at too great length on physical defects and the mincing ridiculous smirking mannerism of a young bride (*The Wedding March,* 1927), or on the cold-blooded affair between a fake country gentleman and a starlet who flopped (*Wives* 1921); to believe one is a sex fiend because one indulges in nothing more vicious than a taste for female undergarments (*Queen Kelly,* 1928; *The Merry Widow,* 1927), is to be rather confused. Stroheim often rescues these vulgarities by an undeniable power of language, but because of that to make of him a kind of evil archangel is to ignore the vast gulf between sadism and caddishness.

For even less worthy reasons, Alfred Hitchcock has acquired an entirely undeserved reputation. The darling sin of this sometimes clever director, capable of smoothly putting together agreeable adventure films, is systematic, militant woman-hating, not even concealed by adequate subtlety. He can in this way present a gallery of mistreated heroines, rich in quantity, even if not outstanding in quality nor variety. Under his direction, Virginia Walles (*Pleasure Garden*, 1925), Annie Ondra (*Blackmail*, 1929), Nova Pilbeam (*The Man Who Knew Too Much*, first version, 1934), Madeline Carroll (*The 39 Steps*, 1935), Sylvia Sidney (*Sabotage*, 1936), Joan Fontaine (*Rebecca*, 1940, *Suspicion*, 1941), Teresa Wright (*Shadow of a Doubt*, 1943), and above all, Ingrid Bergman (*Spellbound*, 1945, *Notorious*, 1946, *Capricorn Lovers*, 1949) and then Grace Kelly (*Dial M For Murder*, 1954; *Rear Window*, 1955; *To Catch a Thief*, 1956), leading to the consecration of Tippi Hedren (*The Birds*, 1962), make up — whatever their beauty and talent otherwise might be or might have been — a monotonous gallery of degraded and insipid females. Nothing is spared them; neither poison, nor terror, nor disembowlment. They are systematically dominated by a murderous or homosexual husband, by a mad Don Juan or by a vindicative governess. Nor do they fail to deserve this — they are fools, liars or betrayers. Hitchcock confuses, for his repulsive ethical purposes, sadism and misogyny.

Despite a painstakingly elaborate censure, that would like, apart from Bresson and Renoir, to consign to outer darkness French cinema prior to May 13, 1958, the case of Henri-Georges Clouzot should be considered with relative sympathy. With a better gift for suspense than Alfred Hitchcock because he has less contempt for his heroes and his audience, Clouzot has been able to give many scenes of violence a most remarkably chilling and climactic atmosphere. Capable of recounting so-called 'perversions', he has organized them into a grandly coherent whole. Cruelty in scenes of crushing, in *Wages of Fear*, the taste for submission, in the same film, psychic or physical torment (*Diabolique,* 1954, or *The Spies,* 1957) are merely ingredients mixed haphazardly, for strictly commercial ends. Lesbianism, even pederasty, are, when necessary, at the service of a perhaps degraded form (but one whose contours are still clear) of passionate love. In his finest film, *Manon* (1949), where the scenarist, Jean Ferry's, contribution is also outstanding, violence and sordidness are transformed by his vision. As Cecile Aubry tells it: "Nothing is disgusting when there is love." The denouement, when, under the desert sun, Michel Auclair, buries his beloved but frees the curve of her face before stretching himself out to die beside her, elevates necrophilia to heights which it never attained except among the romantics or in "Juliette".

Blood of the Beasts (1949), with its rows of butchered, but twitching sheep, its placid slaughterers capable of killing a steer with a single accurate blow of a cleaver, or of splitting it in two to the rhythm of the twelve strokes of noon, is enough to rank Georges Franju among the pitiless. The choice of ridiculous horror, and the exact description of warrior weapons in *Hotel Des Invalides* (1951), the clinical depicting of disease in *Small Change* (1954), and *The Curies* (1953), like the diffusing blood in *Atlantic Salmon* (1955), support this classification. And his two earliest full-length films, both *Head Against the Wall,* where within the high-walled world of a mental hospital, the bills are paid to the discordant pealing of bells, and saws buzzing, and *Faceless Eyes,* where the decomposition of living flesh helps the clinical removal of facial skin, and gulping dogs fight over their victim, would not seem to invalidate it. Finally, use of the haunted chateau ratifies this judgment. Franju, himself, was — to use the absurd cliche — "a disciple of the divine Marquis". There is nothing more premature than these deductions. Franju's too-scrupulous tenderness, his vigilant hatred of every species of enslavement, should have led him at a thousand points to a morality simultaneously too humane and freedom-loving and yet too austere and rigorous to satisfy its lazy relative. This is no way detracts from his talent. It is permissible not to be sadistic, but not permissible to attribute adjectives wrongly and perversely.

The most subtle distinctions occur in the best works. "Fisher's work," Michel Caen wrote accurately, "appears as one of the most sadistic — I do not say Sadean — and cruellest in the modern cinema. Behind chateau walls, instincts are given free rein. It is therefore normal that violence and cruelty rule there as masters, derived from and fulfillments of a too-long suppressed sexual drive." For whoever balks at this superlative, Caen offers *The Stranglers of Bombay* (1959): "As far back as the scene before the credit-lines, a young boy, during an initiation ceremony, has his right arm pierced by a dagger, then carefully cauterized by a red-hot iron, while an assistant collects the blood in a little cup."

"Two wretched people, who, if I may put it this way, are strangled for their own pleasure, have their tongues pulled out and their eyes poked out by a torturer who delicately handles a full assortment of little hooks brought to red heat in glowing embers."

"Then, in the course of a scene of rare cruelty, the two condemned ones, mute, blind, their faces spotted with clots of blood, are finally strangled before the assembled cultists."

"A young Hindu woman, whose maddening bosom, incredibly exposed, streams with sweat, contemplates the corpse with obvious pleasure."

"It is necessary to mention Guy Rolfe, crucified in the sun, his thigh slashed open so that the blood will attract a phallic cobra, the exhumations, the cut-off hands which are tossed, at night, into English houses as a warning . . . it would be

necessary to cite almost the entire film, frame by frame."
("Midi-Minuit Fantastique," No. 1, p. 10.)

Even though his genius shows some unevenness, it is again
necessary to refer to Richard Fleischer. His earliest films
permitted in France brought proof of a very sure flair for the
disturbing threat. Even more than in the story of the un-
willing decoy (*Trapped,* 1949), the killers, methodically
patrolling the corridors of the train in *The Narrow Margin*
(1952), are the unmistakable signs of this disposition. After
the fairly insipid *Arena,* whose rodeos were not as good as
Nicholas Ray's, Fleischer begins to hit his stride in freeing
the crustaceans and giant devilfish of *20,000 Leagues Under
the Sea* (1955), and in making James Mason's Captain
Nemo haughty, misanthropic and aloof from society in the
baroque splendor of his Nautilus. Then came *Bandido* (1956),
where Robert Mitchum, Gilbert Roland and Ursula Thiess
formed a triangle of humor, cruelty and passion equally
chilling. The little-known but splendid *Girl on the Red Velvet
Swing* (1955) was a high point. Jean Collins, stunningly
radiant, nested in the splendor of turn of the century decor;
there was the conflict of Ray Milland's passion and Farley
Granger's mad jealousy, both wanting only to confine her
in the privileged place of their desires. The end of the film
vastly surpasses, in the terms of moral horror, the debatable
Lola Montez by Ophuls. *The Vikings* ranks high in the filmography of climactic scenes. The confrontation between one-
armed Tony Curtis and one-eyed Kirk Douglas makes superiority in cruelty the *sine qua non* for equal status, in a world
where one cuts off the braids of unfaithful wives while flinging
axes at random; where guilty slaves are subject to the ordeal
of the sea, and where sorcerers raise the wind that stops the
tide. After these high points, I cite to the advantage of the
second that it is, besides, illuminated by Janet Leigh's beauty,

These Thousand Hills (1959), and *Drama in a Mirror* (1961), despite the violence of the first and the interesting variation on the theme of the "double" in the second, they are clearly a retreat. *Barabbas* (1961), finally would be a quite dismaying descent to the biblical if some flashes of cruelty: the stoning of Sylvana Mangano, a mine collapsing, a savage fight between Anthony Quinn and Jack Palance, a final crucifixion, were not there to cheer up the Fleischer fans.

Bunuel Meets De Sade

While everywhere else sadism in the cinema is either just the result of chance encounters of fancies, or really the fruit of benevolent luck in picking stories, the work of Luis Bunuel offers the unique example of awareness and perfect understanding of Sade. As far from a photo copy as from a surrender unacceptable on principle, this is a most exhilarating and rich confrontation.

The denouement of his second film, *L'Age d'Or* (*The Golden Age*), in 1930, established the exact register marks. The only absolutely explicit reference to sadism in the history of the cinema, its script deserves to be reproduced at length:

"237 . . . Vertical panorama rising until it discloses a mountain, abrupt and enormous, covered with snow. At the edge of a precipice the threatening silhouette of a medieval chateau rears up.

"A long shot of the chateau.

"A long shot of the front with its gate closed.

"Subtitle (in double exposure with falling feathers). 'AT THE EXACT MOMENT WHEN THESE FEATHERS, TORN OUT BY HIS FURIOUS HANDS, COVERED THE EARTH AT THE BASE OF THE WINDOW — AT THAT MOMENT, WE SAY, BUT FAR AWAY, THE SURVI-

VORS OF THE CHATEAU DE SELLINY WERE SET-
TING OFF TO RETURN TO PARIS TO CELEBRATE
THE MOST BRUTAL OF ORGIES, THEY HAD BEEN
LOCKED UP, 120 DAYS PREVIOUSLY, THESE FOUR
THOROUGH-GOING, UNMISTAKABLE SCOUNDRELS,
WHO HAVE NO GOD BUT THEIR LUST, NO LAW
BUT THEIR DEPRAVITY, NO BRAKE BUT THEIR
DEBAUCHERY, LIBERTINES WITHOUT GOD, WITH-
OUT PRINCIPLES, WITHOUT RELIGION, THE LEAST
CRIMINAL OF THEM DEFILED BY MORE WICKED-
NESS THAN YOU COULD POSSIBLY ENUMERATE, IN
WHOSE EYES THE LIFE OF A WOMAN — WHAT AM
I SAYING, ONE WOMAN, ALL THE WOMEN ON THE
FACE OF THE EARTH — IS AS TRIVIAL A THING
AS SWATTING A FLY. THEY BROUGHT WITH THEM
INTO THE CHATEAU, SOLELY TO SERVE THEIR
FILTHY DESIGNS, EIGHT MARVELOUS GIRLS, EIGHT
MAGNIFICENT TEENAGERS, AND, SO THAT THEIR
IMAGINATION (ALREADY CORRUPTED BY EXCESS)
SHOULD BE CONTINUALLY EXCITED, THEY LIKE-
WISE BROUGHT ALONG FOUR DEPRAVED WOMEN
WHO UNCEASINGLY FED THE CRIMINAL SENSU-
ALITY OF THE FOUR MONSTERS WITH THEIR
STORIES. HERE NOW LEAVING THE CHATEAU DE
SELLINY ARE THE SURVIVORS OF THESE CRIMINAL
ORGIES; THE FOUR ORGANIZERS AND LEADERS —
THE DUC DE BLANGY

"238. Close-up of the portal, which opens very slowly as
if the rust of its hinges were holding it back. The haloed
head of a man appeared, with beard and mustache, dressed
in the manner of Hebrews of the first century of our era.

"239. A slightly longer shot to allow a full-length view of
the Duc de Blangy. His eyes, half-closed after the great

prison, are dazzled by the snow-glare. He looks behind him to see if anyone is following, and proceeds forward.

"Subtitle:

PRESIDENT CURVAL AND FINANCIER DURCET

"One after the other, they come out, one dressed in the Oriental manner of fourth century B.C., the other like an ordinary Arab (sixth century A.D.). Both, after noting the course taken by the leader go in that direction.

"Subtitle:

THE REMAINING ONE OF THE FOUR:
THE BISHOP OF K

"The last character comes limping out, dressed like a 16th century priest. He heads in the same direction as the others. All should come out and walk rapidly.

"240. Background shot of the first character near a snow-covered rock, in the attitude of someone waiting for another, in order to start out at once. The others come into the shot and without saying a word go close to the first, similiarly waiting for the remaining one.

"241. Long shot of the portal which has remained ajar. For a while, the portal by itself.

"A little girl of about 13, on the doorstep, terrorized, dressed in a big chemise, holding her bosom with one of her hands at the place corresponding to one of her breasts, covered with bloodstains.

"242. She has fallen exhausted on the very threshold; the last of the characters re-enters the scene and, taking the little girl in his arms, carries her into the chateau. Pause, during which nothing unusual occurs, except a great, terrifying scream from the interior; a few moments later, the same character, impassive, goes to join the rest, accordingly leaving the scene.

"243. A deep white snow . . . Lashed by the snow and the

wind, moving one after the other at the right of the scene, coming up to a long shot (let the actors walk up an inclined ramp), are the four impassive characters.

"From above — a snow-covered cross covered with locks of women's hair, cruelly blown about by the wind whitened with snow."

Although in certain details (the subtitles are shorter, the scene less cut-up; only the Duc de Blangy is dressed as a "Hebrew"*, the others in 18th century garb; it is Blangy who finally finishes off the little girl) the film itself does differ from the original script, the full quotation is not the less revealing. It establishes the relationship between Sade and Bunuel; it sets the most necessary reference of the shot immediately at the level of scandal. Society was not deceived by it. To the statements by the "Journal General de France": "Everything that the most disordered imagination could conceive, in the way of indecency, sophistry, even the revolting, is piled up in this bizarre novel (*Justine, or the Misfortunes of Virtue*), whose title could intrigue and deceive sensitive and respectable souls" in 1792, and by the very civic minded "Ami des Lois" — "The very name of this infamous writer exhales a corpse-like odor that kills virtue and inspires horrors", in 1799, correspond (in 1930) the articles in, this time, L'Ami du peuple", and "Figaro": "A film entitled *L'Age d'Or,* in which I defy any expert to recognize the least artistic value, multiplies in a public exhibition the most obscene, the most repugnant, and the most wretched episodes. Fatherland, Family and Religion are there dragged through dung." Or in L'Echo de Paris": "This pretentious and bleak imposition has no relationship with avantgarde art, nor with art at all."

---

*The synopsis of the program, as a precaution, dotted its "i's": "The Duc de Blangy is evidently Jesus Christ."

Despite lack of intelligence, of taste, in fact, of culture, to which neither the oldest nor the youngest of these con- temners could pretend, it is necessary to concede to them an intuition. Like Sade, Bunuel shocks and maddens. Thus he automatically fascinates, or else why the frightened and hypocritical defense by appealing to inverted logic: "if he hates religion so much, it is because *at bottom* he believes," or even the scientific, geographical explanation, the recourse to "spirit of the people": "all that is so very Spanish. More specifically, Aragonese", or even the blackmail pressure, that was brutally manifested by the "Ligue des patriotes," and continued slyly for almost 20 years of his creative semi- retirement. Similarly, nowadays, Sade is excused and ex- plained away by psychiatrists and Christians, though he spent almost his entire life in prison.

Bunuel depicts violence because it is violence; his scenes awake it with the utmost ease. The notorious opening sequence in his first film (*Andalusian Dog*) is, as everyone knows, the one in which an eye is cut in two by a razor stroke. Arturo de Cordova, in *He* (1952), afraid of being spied upon by a voyeur when in a hotel room with his young bride, Delia Garces, coldly thrusts a long knitting-needle through the keyhole. Georges Merchal, in (*Death in the Garden*, 1956), has a priest (Michel Piccoli) bring him pen and ink in prison. He thrusts the pen into his jailer's eye and escapes. There are few of his films which do not present at least one flash of pure, almost gratuitous, violence. The blind man knocked down by a thrown rock, and the epileptic seizures of Jaibo, in *The Young and the Damned*, 1950, make social or clinical sense, but the battles among insects in *Robinson Crusoe*, 1952, the scorpions in *L'Age d'Or* (1930), or for that matter the fox slaughtering hens in *The Young Women*, 1959, or even the spike hammered into a back in *The Brute*,

1952, easily go beyond rational explanation.

This show of coolness in the face of suffering parallels an equal impassivity in the face of death. In *Under the Sky* as well as in *The River of Death*, 1954, again, the characters manifest no religious dread before corpses, and we are very far from the morbid descriptions of Bossuet's "Sermon on Death".

Bunuel knows so well to whom he is referring in his scenes that the allusion can become literal. The hero in *He*, mad with a jealousy solicitously supported by religious and social constraints, tortures his wife through an entire night, without anyone becoming alarmed (similarly, in *l'Age d'Or*, a game-warden, for some trivial reason, kills his child with a gunshot, without provoking any reaction but a polite disapproval) gets ready to subject her to the tortures inflicted in "The Bedroom Philosophers" on Mme. de Mistival. He prepares everything necessary for the sewing: needle, razor-blades, thread, string, scissors, cotton and disinfectant.

Bunuel knows, too, that this violence in reality does not actually stir virtuous people who reject it in the name of their morality. It seems scandalous to them only for bad reasons. A father has almost the right to kill his son — the law almost allows it to him — but a slap given to a contemptible old countess arouses general censure. Similarly, Sade, methodical painter of sexual tortures, declared himself, at the height of the Terror, opposed to the death penalty. For one, as for other, violence and cruelty are a challenge. Far indeed from being maniacs at whom one can smile, whom one can disregard or "understand," they are fully aware of true motivations. They are moralists and not moralizers.

And this comprehension goes far beyond the superficial level of cruelty. Even more than at the end of *Age d'Or* or the sewing scene in *He*, in the dialogue in *Robinson Crusoe*

(1952) between Robinson and Friday, it is displayed with verve. Both Ado Kyrou and Freddy Buache have, in their books on Bunuel, analyzed the scene: "Robinson," writes Buache, "is a colonist, and cannot comprehend any other relationship with Friday than that of master to slave . . . He puts chains on him and, a little later, teaches him Christian theology. But Friday reacts with disconcerting wisdom which Bunuel, smiling, equates to that which the dying Sade throws at the priest: 'So your god wanted to make everything amiss, just to test or try out his creature; then he did not understand him; then he was not sure of the result?' " ("Premier Plan" No. 13, pp. 27-28). The reference to "Dialogue" is found still more explicitly in the cholera sequence in *Nazarin,* where the priest cannot draw from the dying girl any other plea than for fleshly love. "What do you want?" — "I want Juan." More certain than ever of what he wants, and of the manner in which he should say it, Bunuel progressively abandons the purely visual scandal of physical violence in favor of the moral scandal of *Nazarin, Viridiana* or *Angel of Death.*

He had, in two films *He* and *The Criminal Life of Archibald of the Cross,* demonstrated the meaning of phantasms. Jealousy, in *He,* was the only outcome (insanity) which religious inhibitions permitted his love. The life of *Archibald* which accumulates futile attempts at sexual murders and many other abortive acts that are the stages of a slow but triumphal liberation, the outcome of which is finally to be able to love, attains the splendid daintiness of sparing an insect's life.

Sade and Bunuel have a final point in common — their romanticism. With the one, as with the other, necrophilia loses its sordid overtones to assert itself as a victory of life over death. The final sequence of *The Summit of Hurlevent* is, as Kyrou wrote ("Le Surrealisme au Cinema," 2nd ed., p. 232), "sublime: imagination, passion, absolute love defying death, all these cherished themes come together in five minutes which are among the most radiant, visually as well as emotionally, which the human spirit has given us."

Like everything Sade wrote, everything Bunuel films is love.

IN CONCLUSION

My friend Louis Seguin often told me how, with Ado Kyrou, he staged marvelous productions. Ava Gardner was a splendid Juliette, and Anthony Quinn a quite passable Minsky. Piccoli did very well as the Duc de Blangy, and the idea of Maria Schell cast as Justine seemed quite amusing to them. Certainly all this was in the realm of dreams, but what could not be done with, say, *Cleopatra* in the perfect freedom of an ideal world! Nearer to this, the silver screen offers, in my view, sparing of shadows and smoke screens, the brute force that can teach that hope is too weak to cling to, except in daydreams.

Censorship exists, threatened or actual, for those who are easily deterred, those for whom The *Briganders* of Jean-Luc Godard is the height of pure anarchism, of virtuosity and of splendid creative freedom. The solicitude to protect youths dedicated to the Johnny Halliday ideal and to moralism for shop girls, the panicking fear of an ethical violence which, if one dared give it its head, would sweep away all those whom you know, and others with them, all these motives raise walls as solid as they are reassuring, to which Roger Vadim has just brought his miserable little brick.

There is no dam so well constructed that, at last, does not

187

allow tiny rivulets to well up, their very unpredictability making them harder to seal off. A red-hot iron here, a flagellation session there, a dungeon or a manhunt, all these little details, preserved by ruses from a censorship luckily blinded by its own stupidity, completed bit by bit, then reassembled, at leisure in personal editing, would result in an ideal film, which everyone might see, fundamentally in opposition to the false health of castration. This book, after all, just wants to help the reader construct for himself, at will, and according to the variations of his own tastes, this ideal film.

Erudition and — let us be modest — mine as well as that of others, having human limitations, I do not doubt that the reader could enrich the list which I have drawn up, from his own research and personal memories. If he will allow me to share it, let him please back up his insults and sarcasms with exact filmographic references. Later editions will follow and, in being more complete, will be enriched.

EXHIBITS
DOCUMENTARY VERIFICATION

P<small>ICTURES</small> *eloquently speak for themselves — but in the selection that follows they also testify to the splendid accuracy of the author's reporting and the psychological keenness of his insights.*

The sequence is alphabetical. The stills generally reflect the climactic scenes of many movies cited in the text. It should, however, be noted that this American edition — while retaining photos that appeared in the French original — has doubled the total number of illustrations by drawing on extensive private collections made available by the kindness of film historians here and abroad.

It remains only to paraphrase the author's concluding remarks: If the reader knows of better illustrative materials he is urged to communicate with the editor — for the enrichment of subsequent editions of SADISM IN THE MOVIES.

BEATING

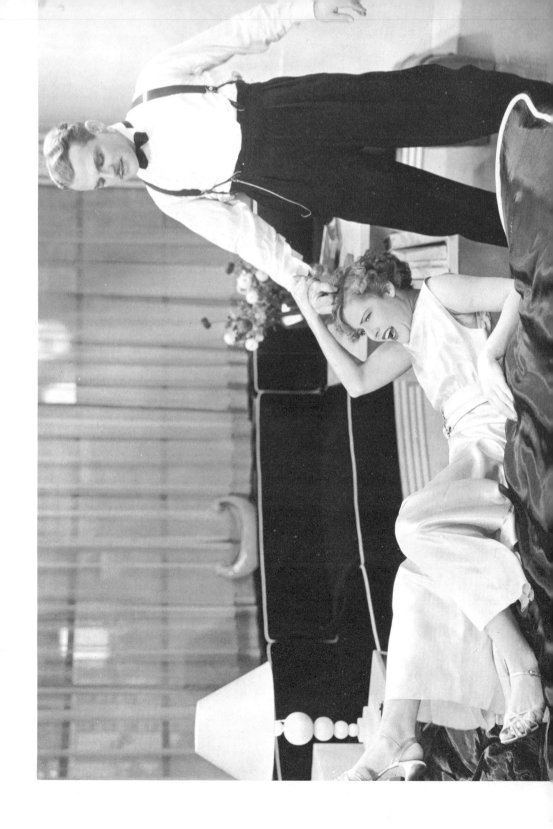

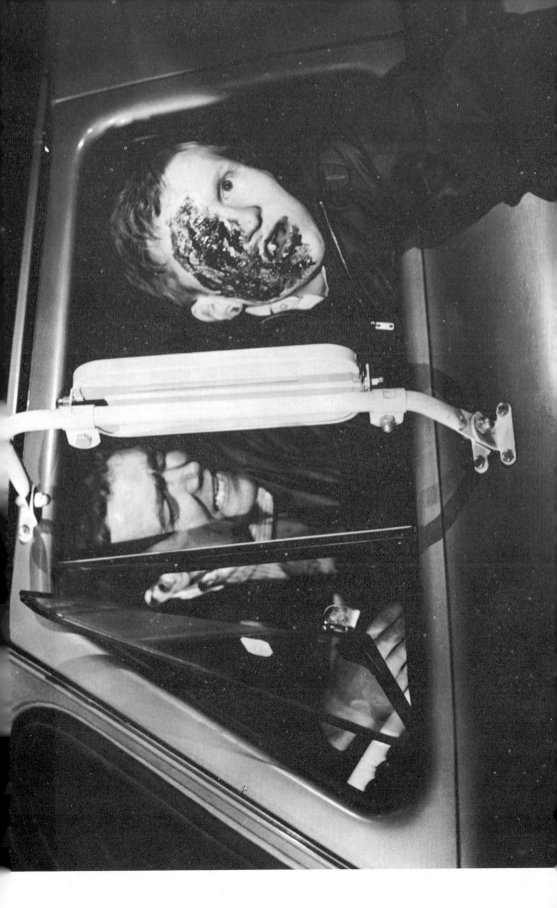

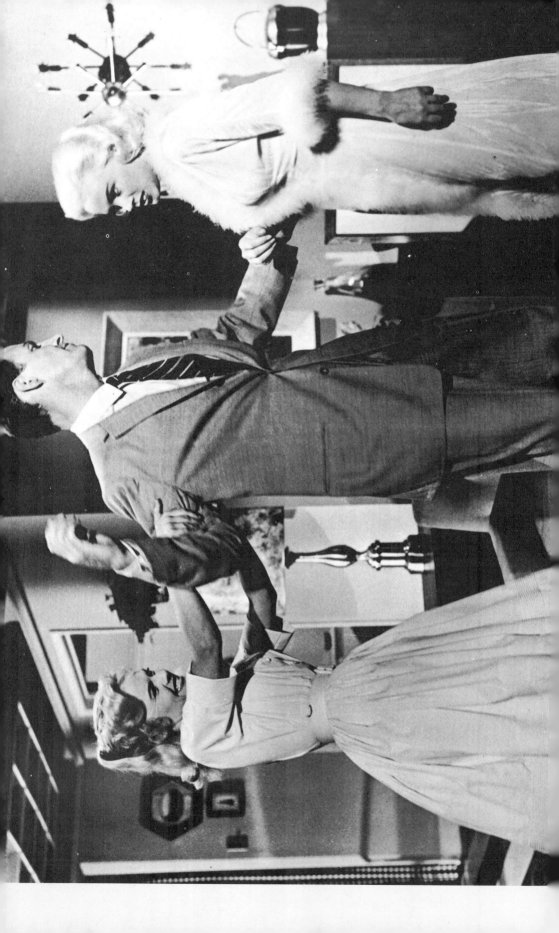

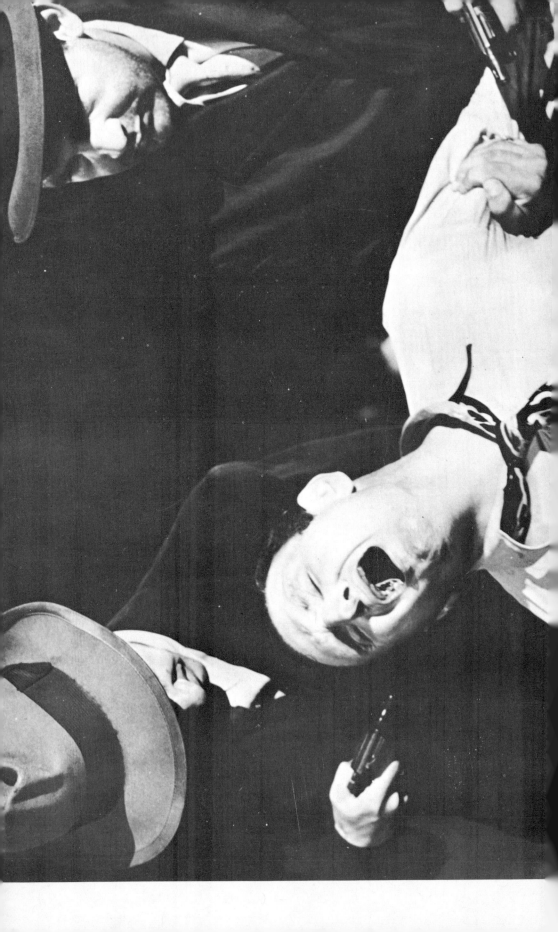

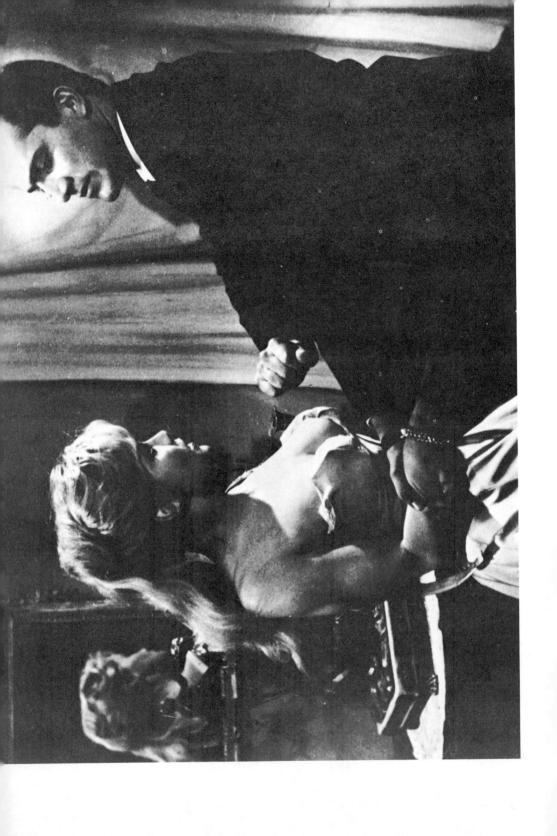

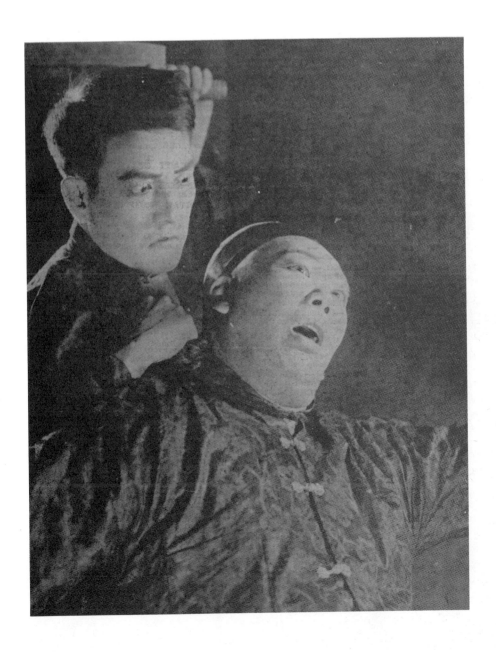

BLOODY DEATH

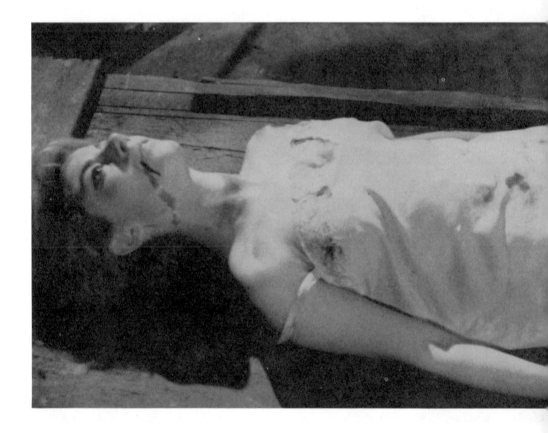

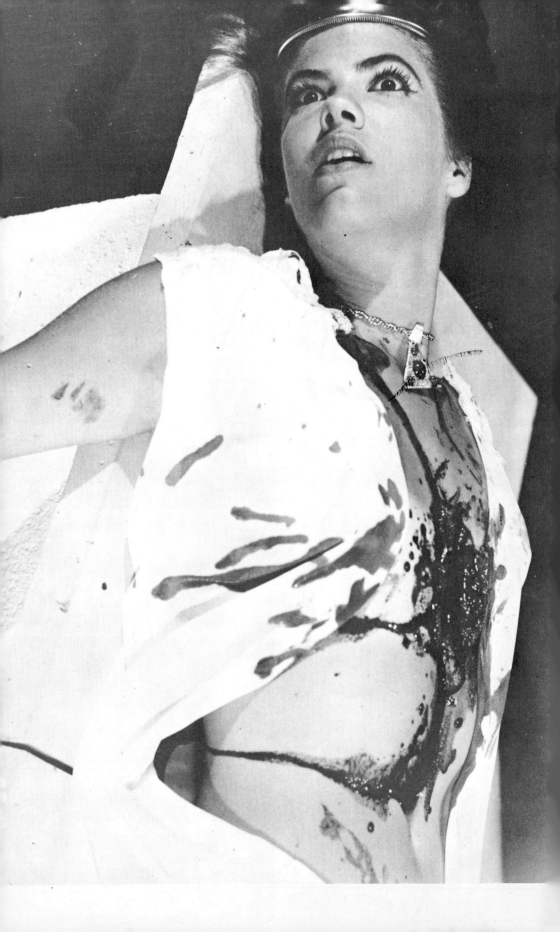

BURNING

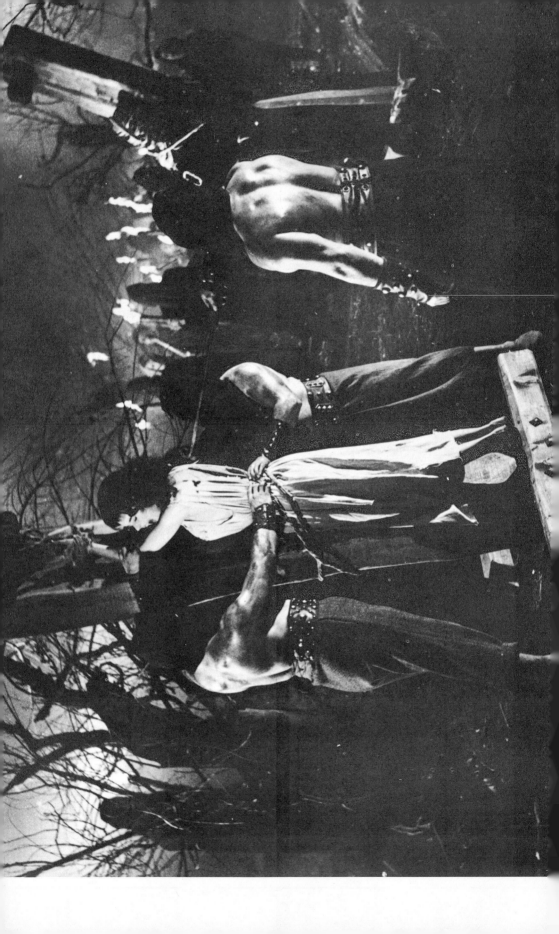

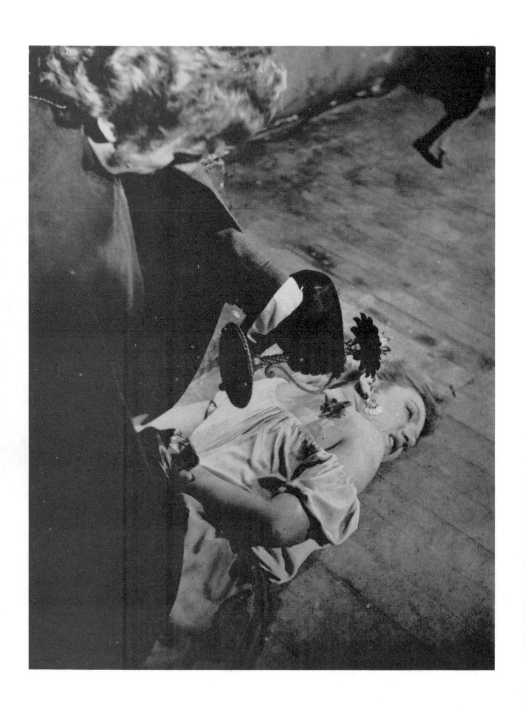

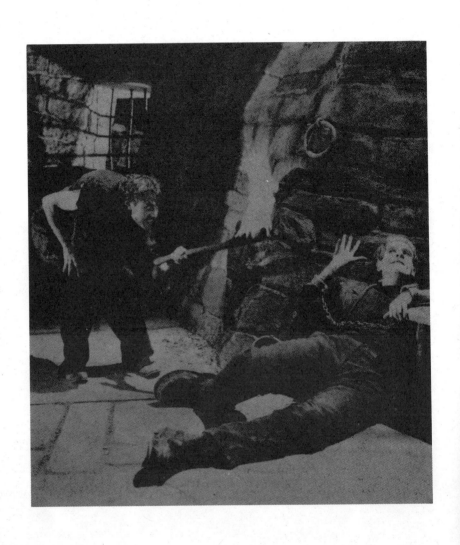

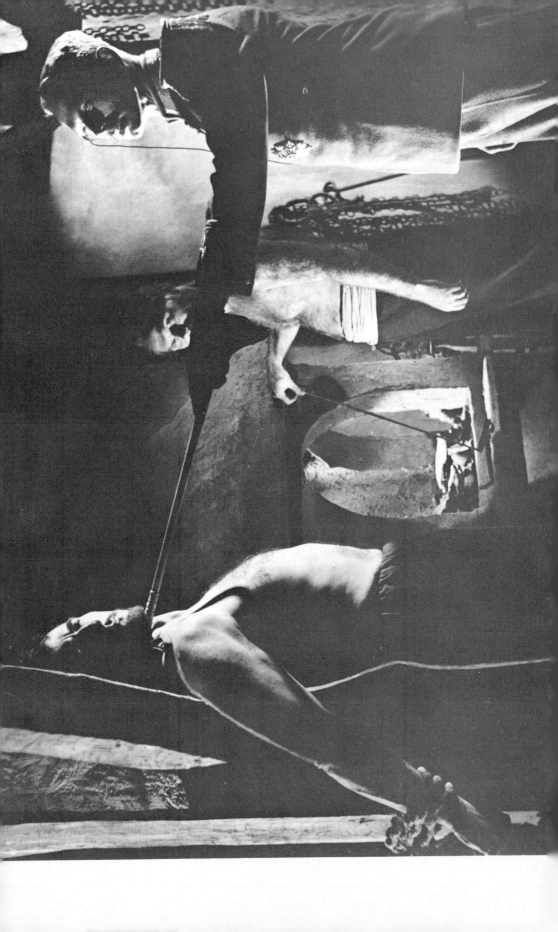

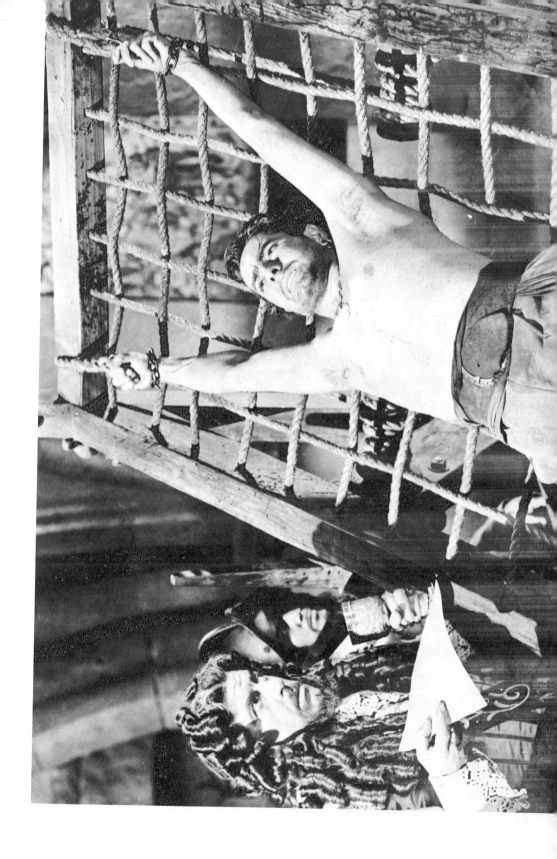

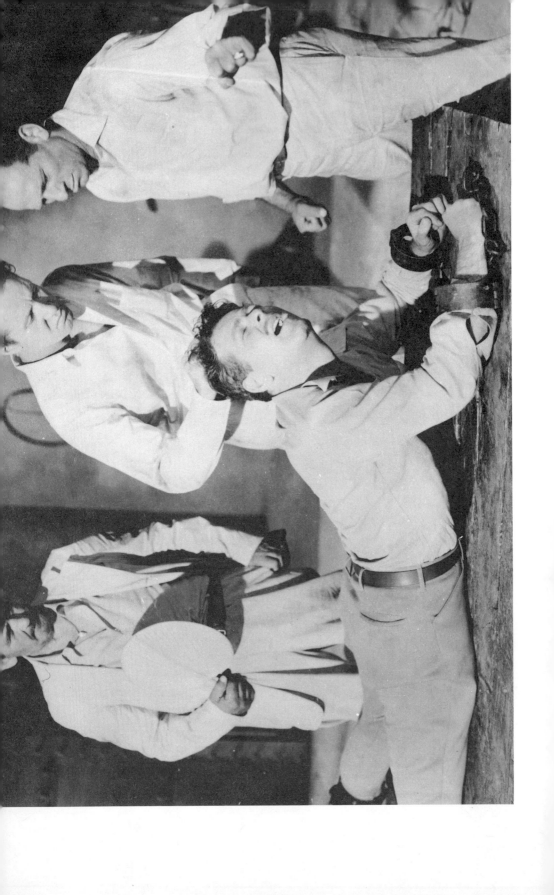

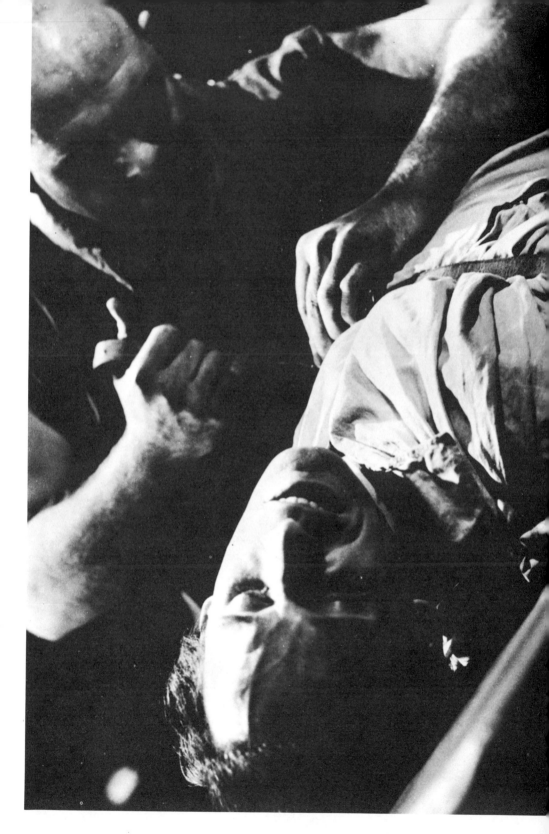

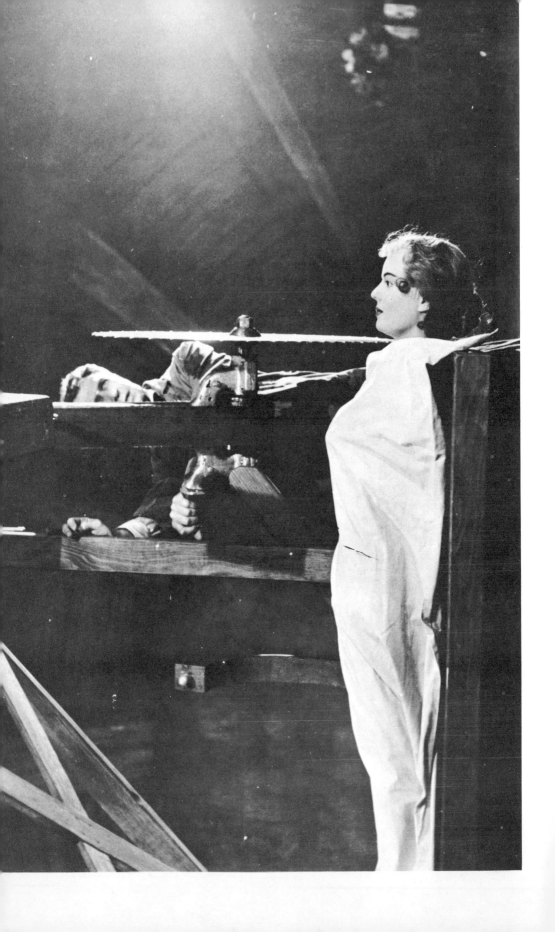

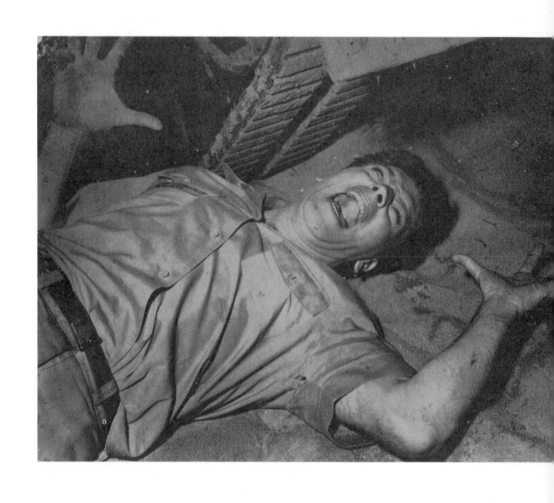

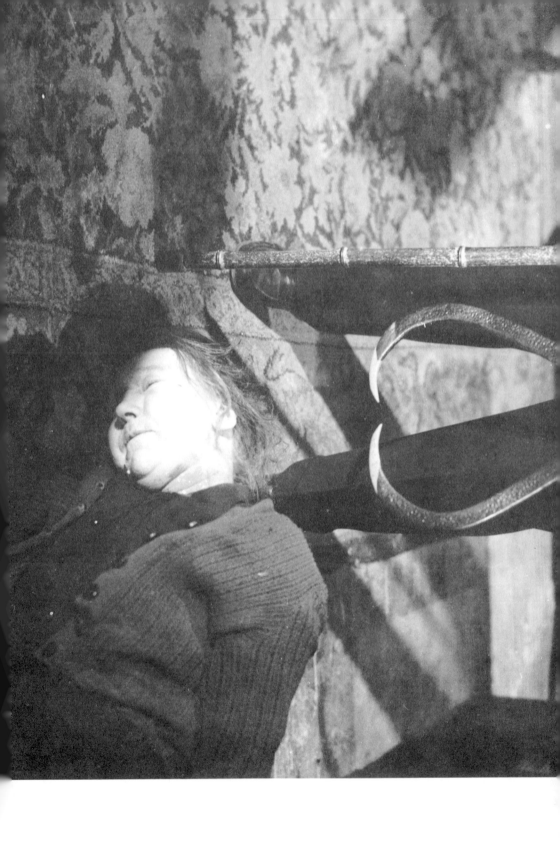

HANGING

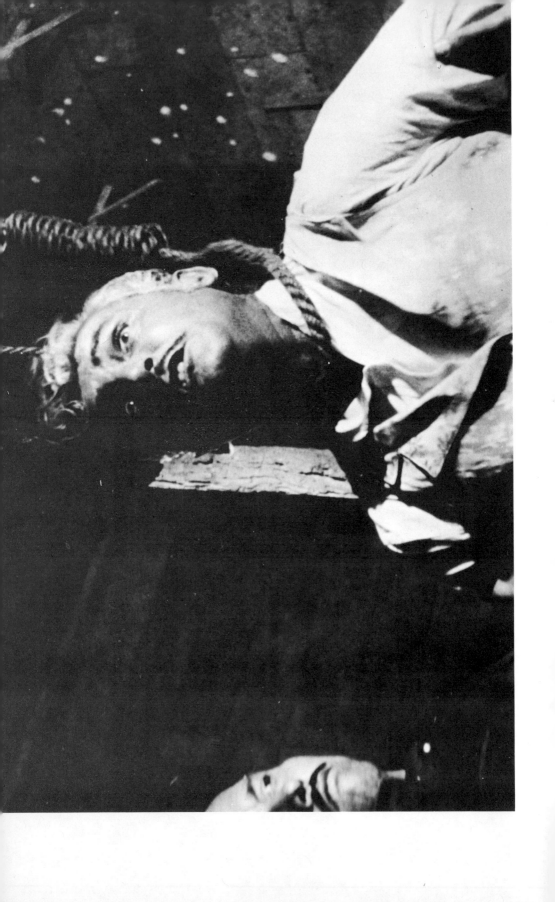

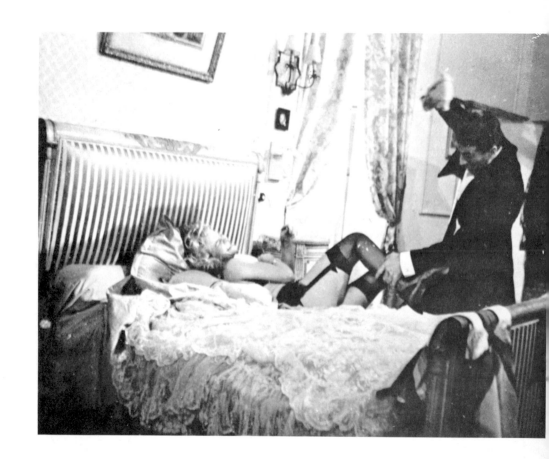

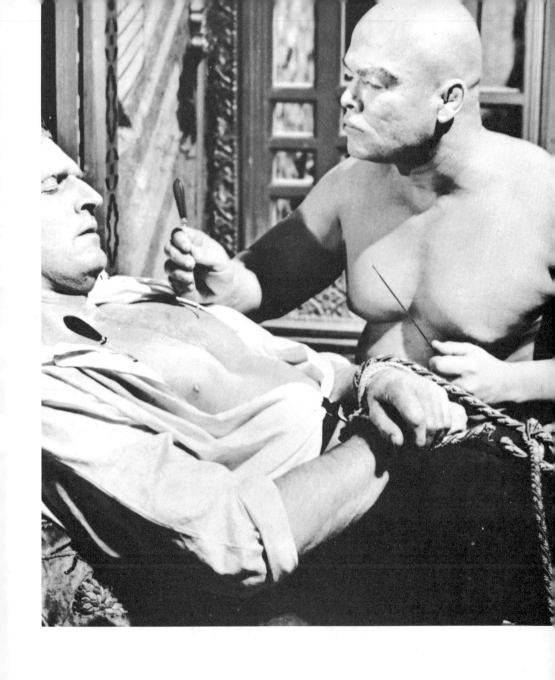

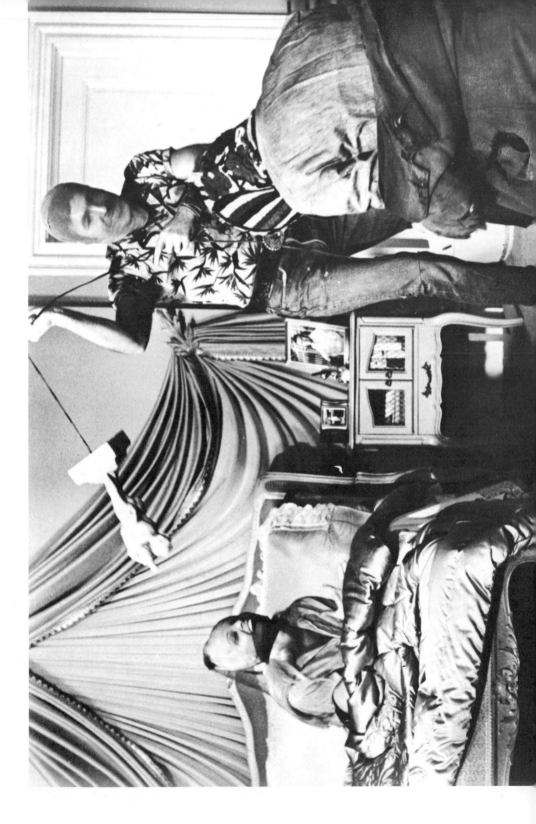

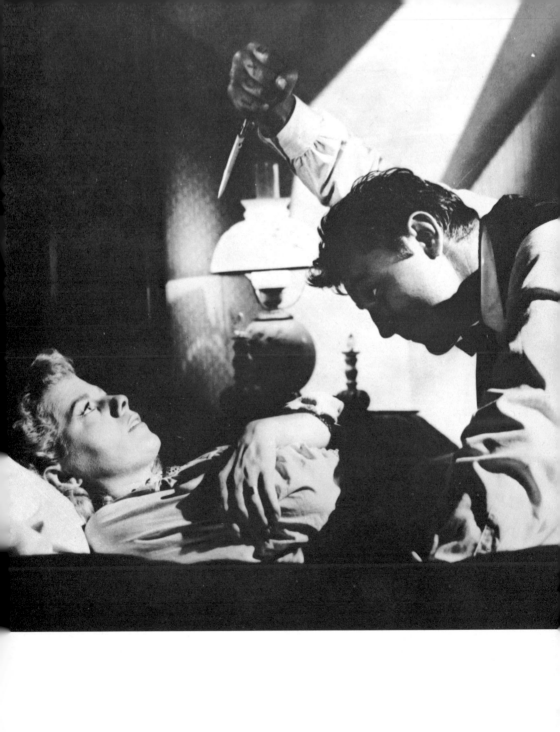

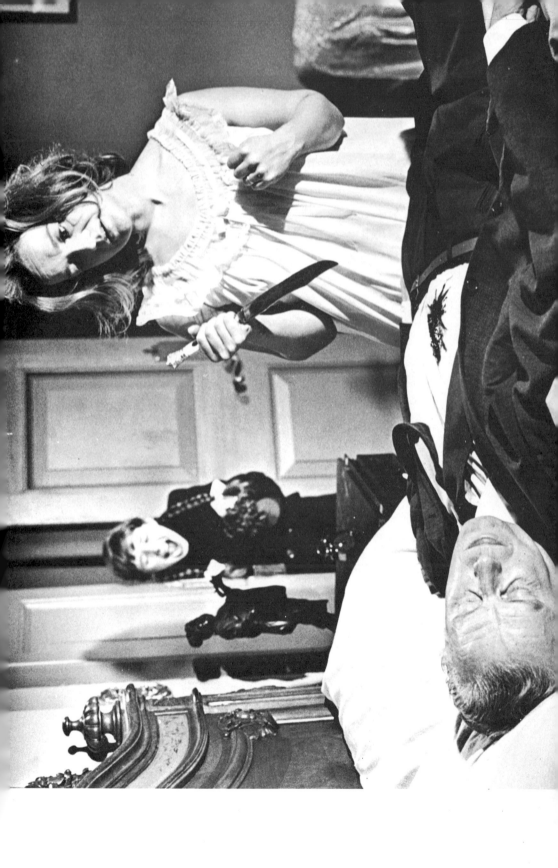

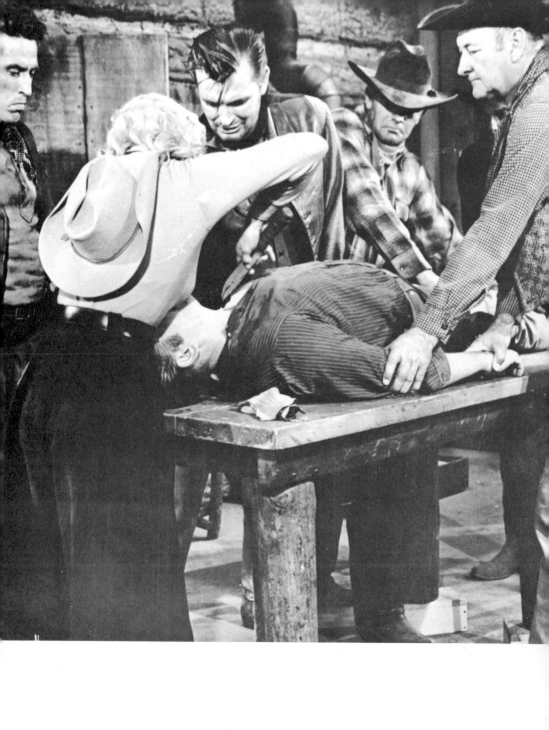

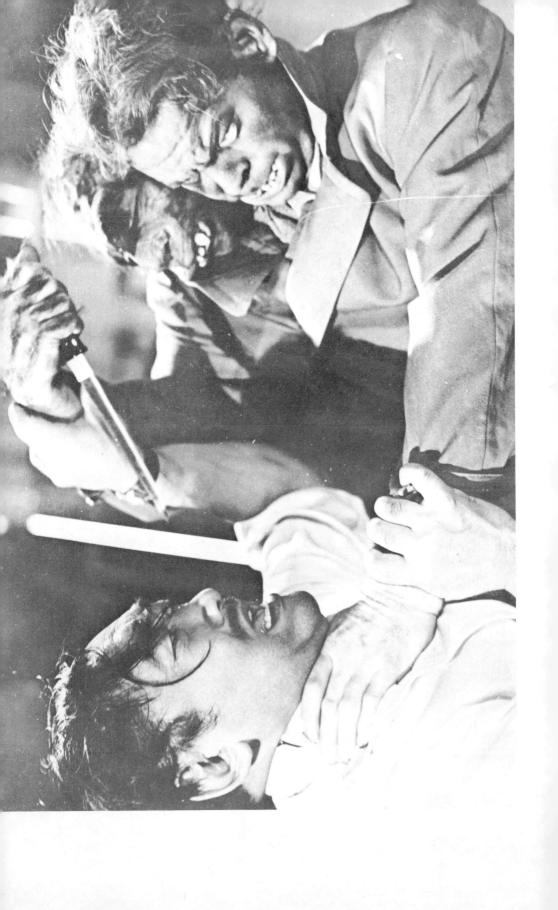

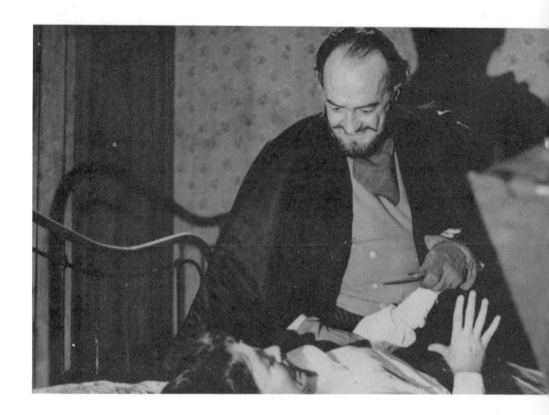

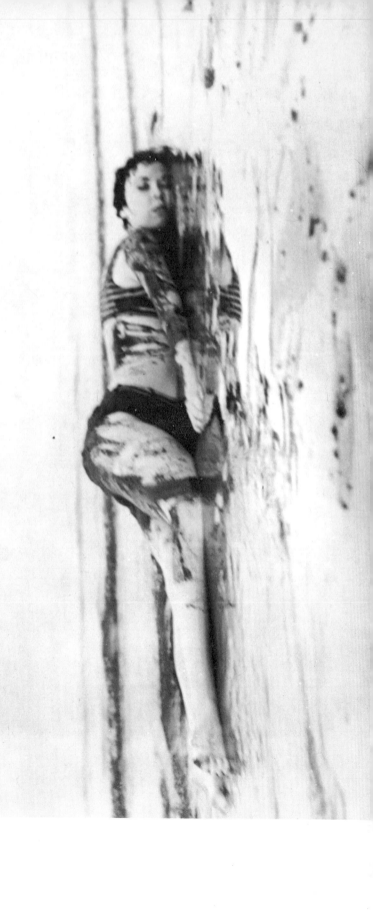

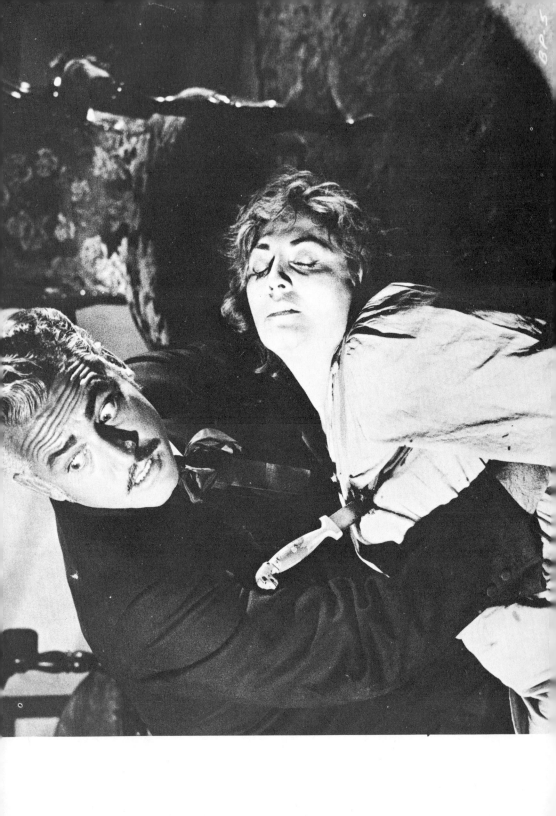

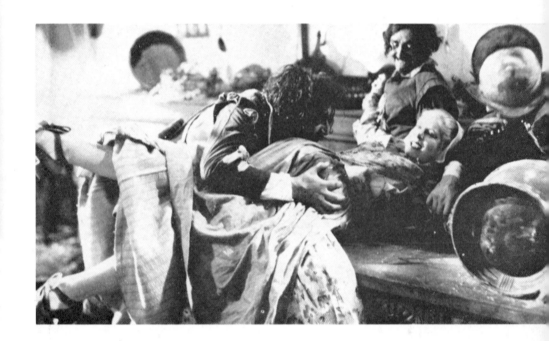

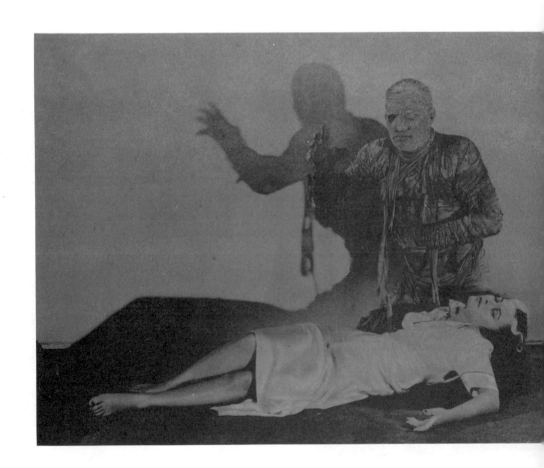

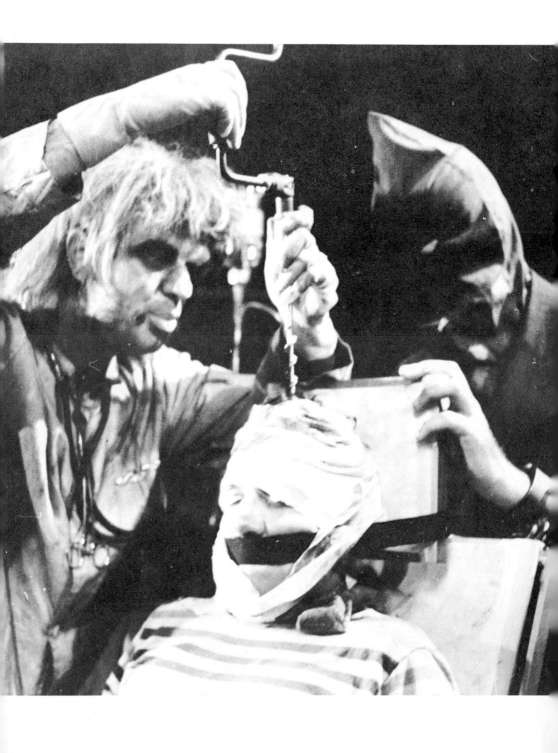

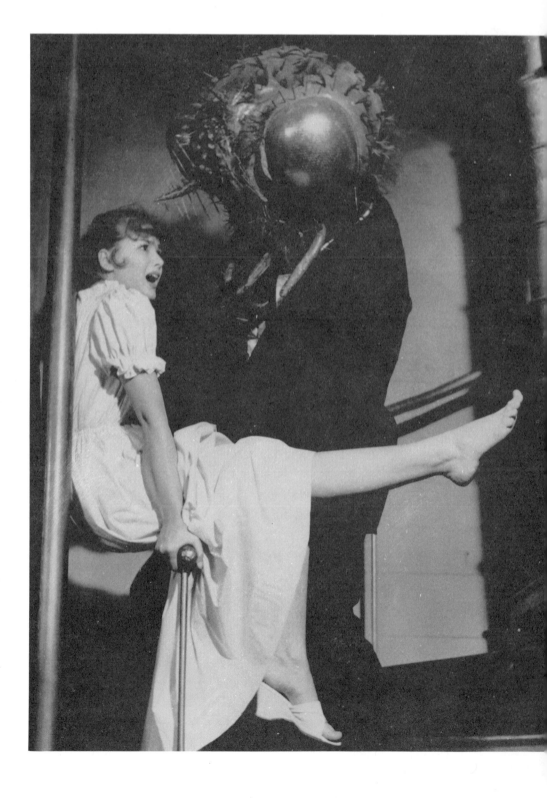

RAPE

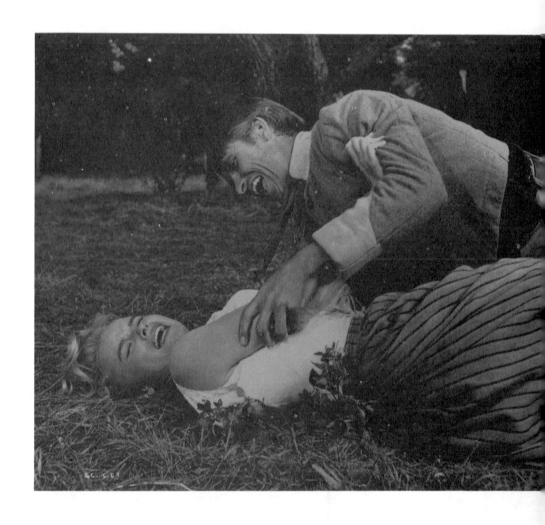

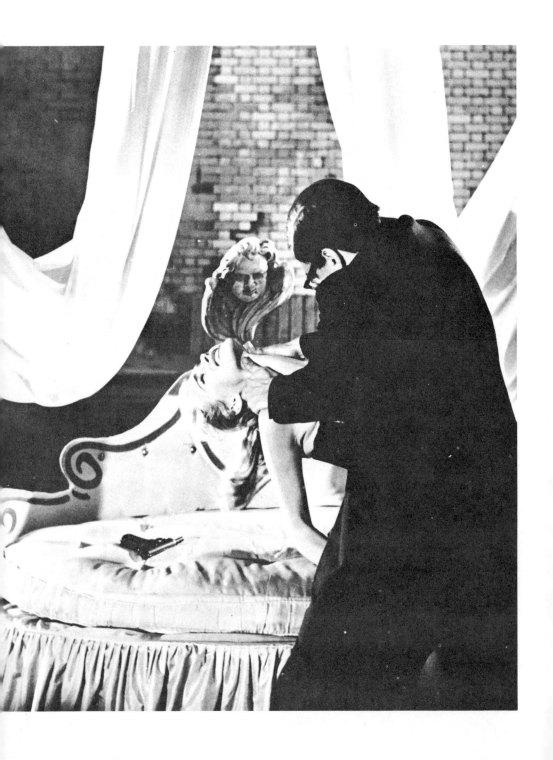

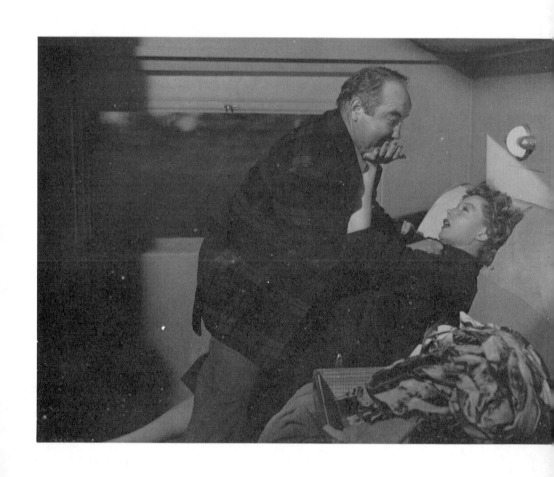

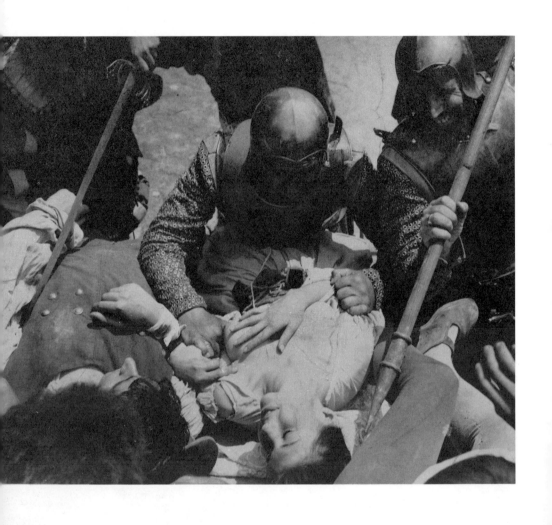

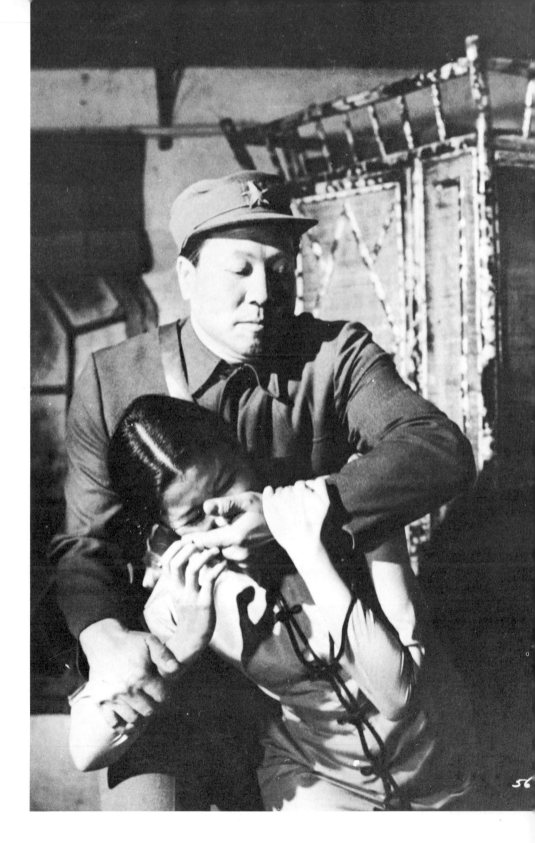

56

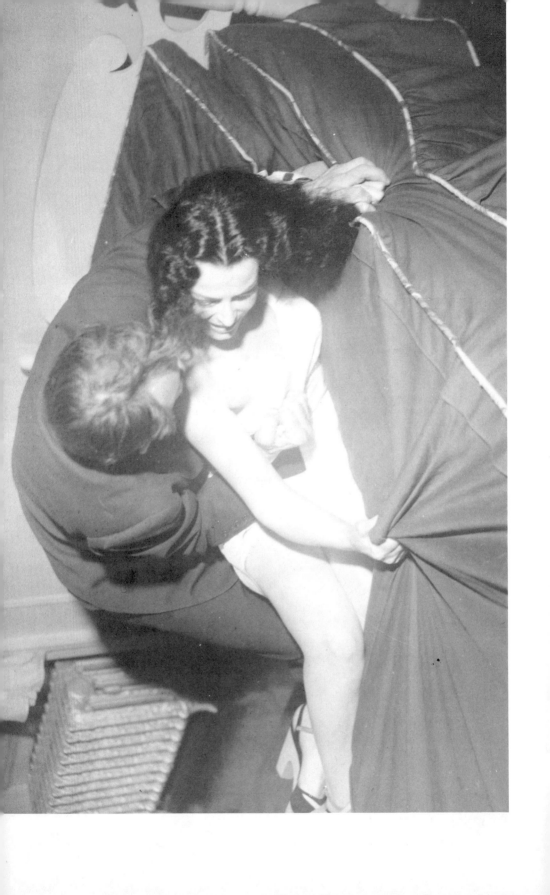

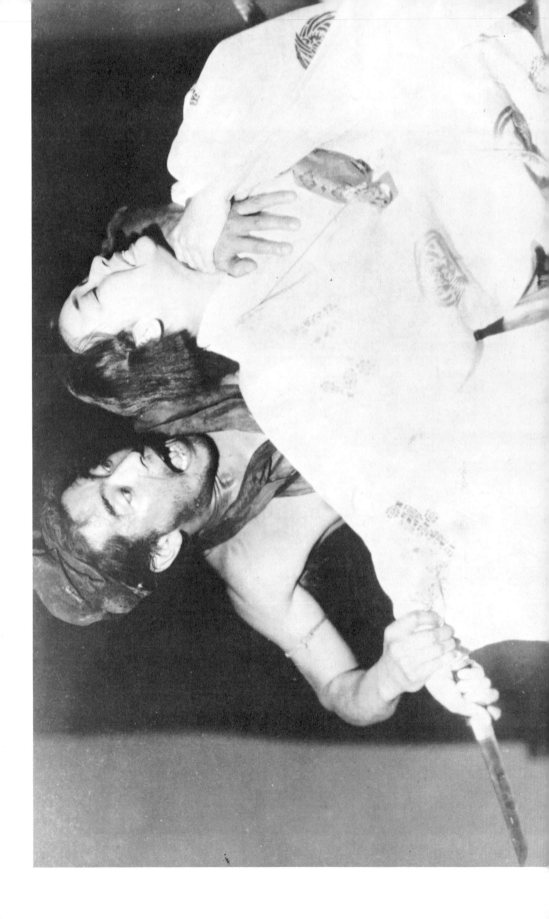

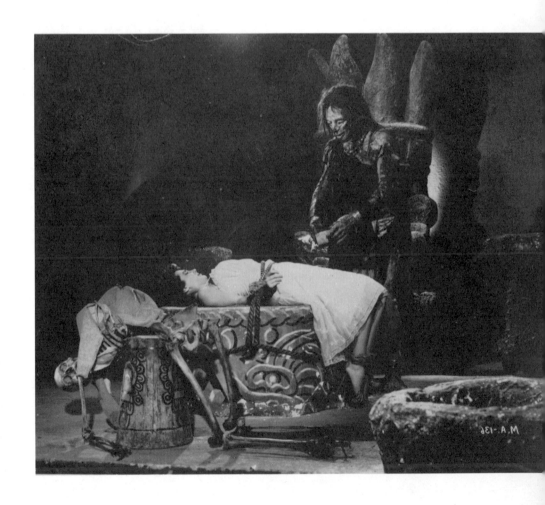

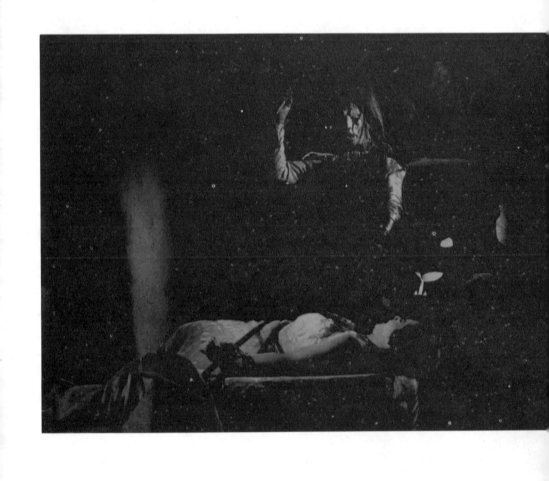

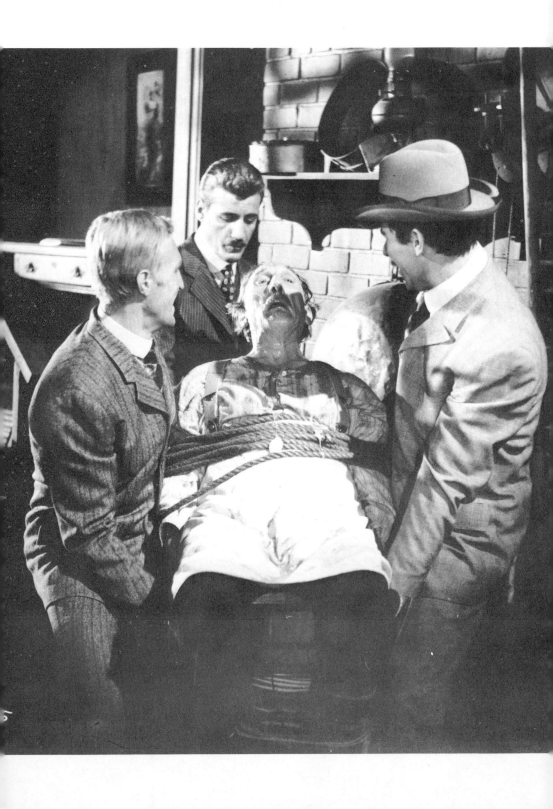

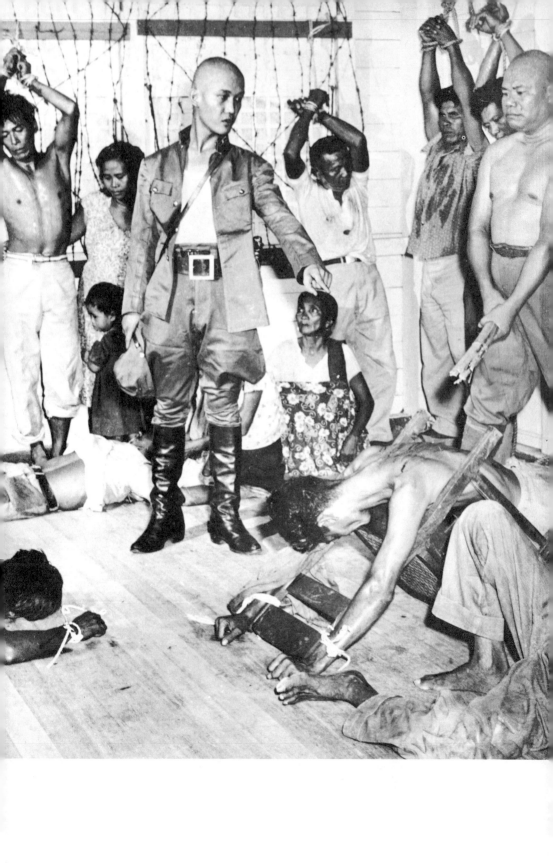

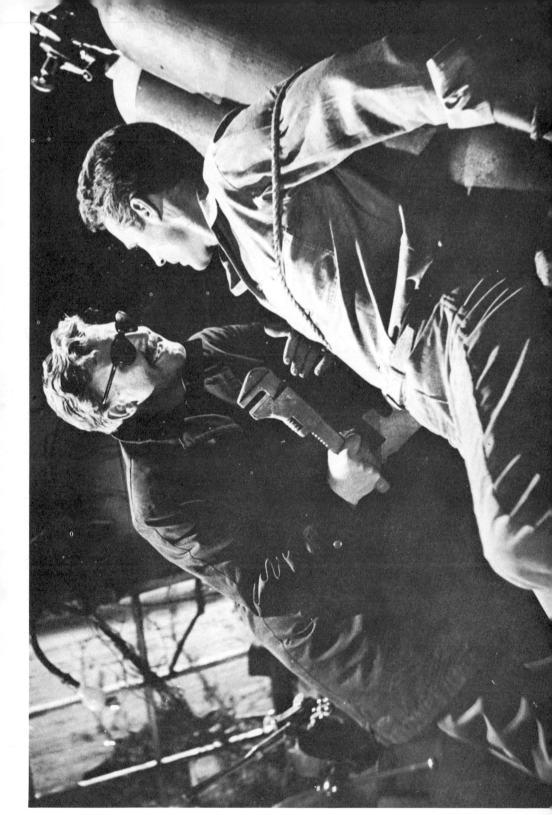

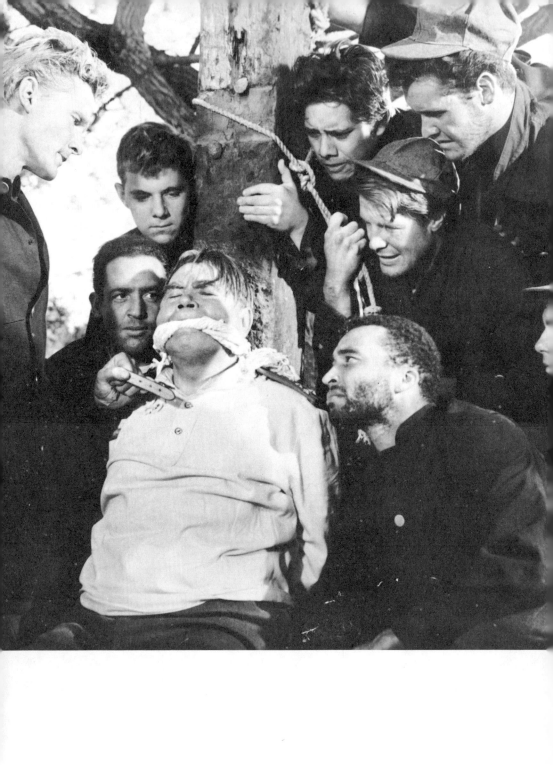

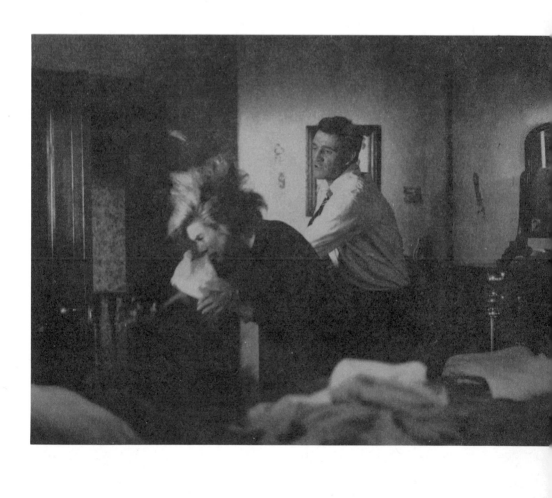

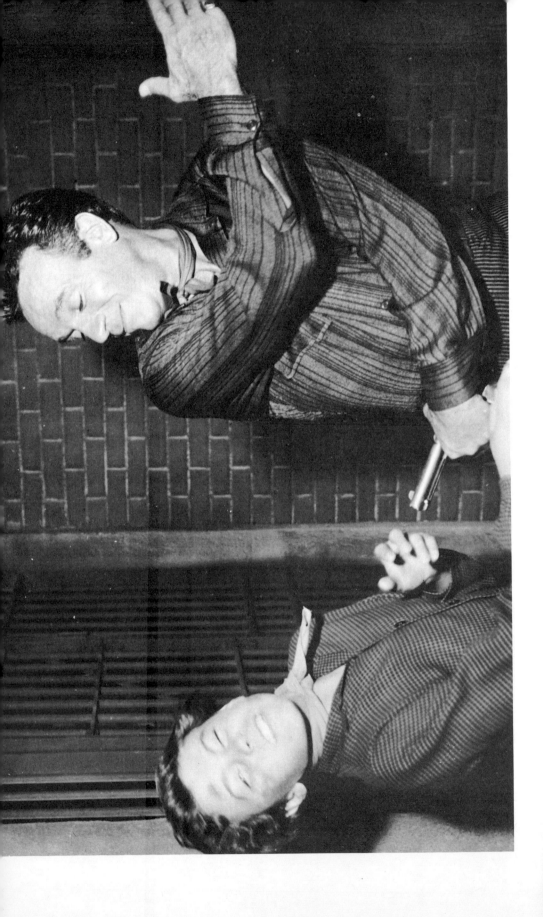

SPANKING

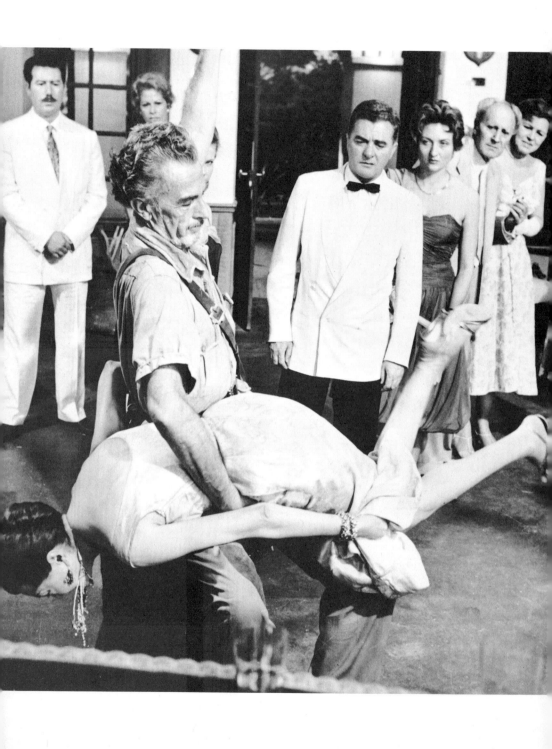

176

STRANGLING

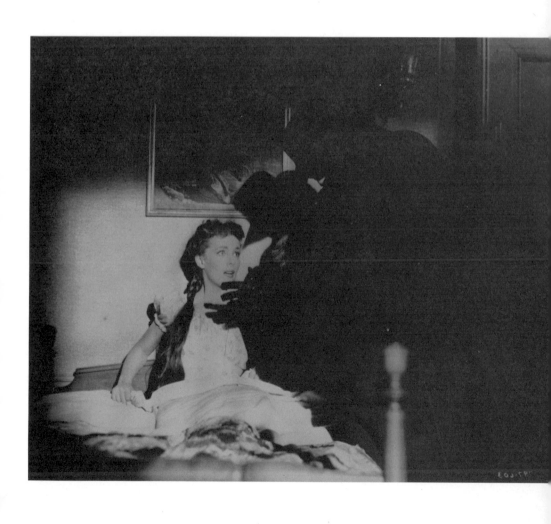

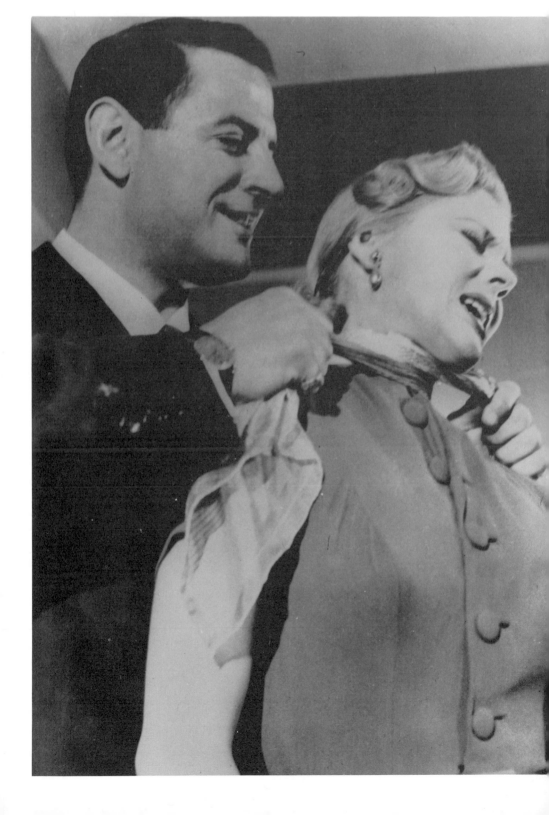

SUBJECTION

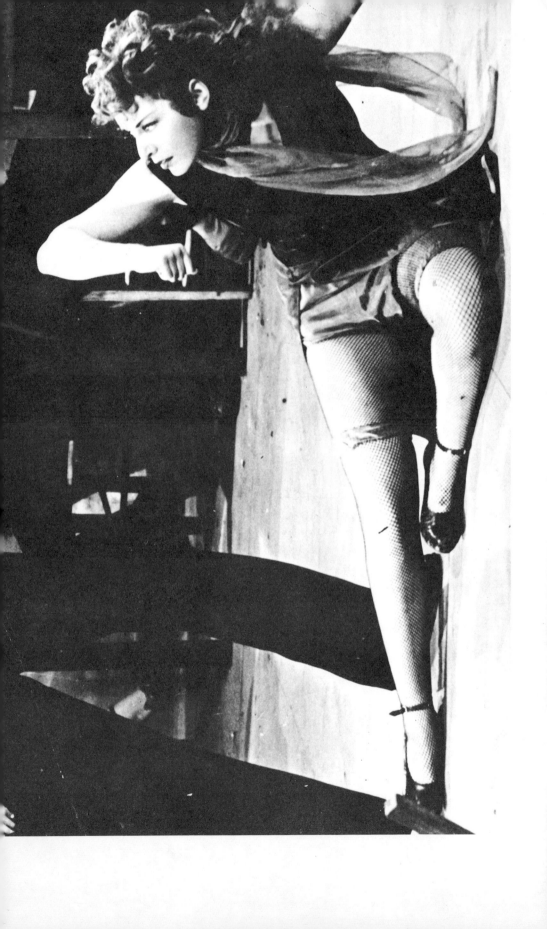

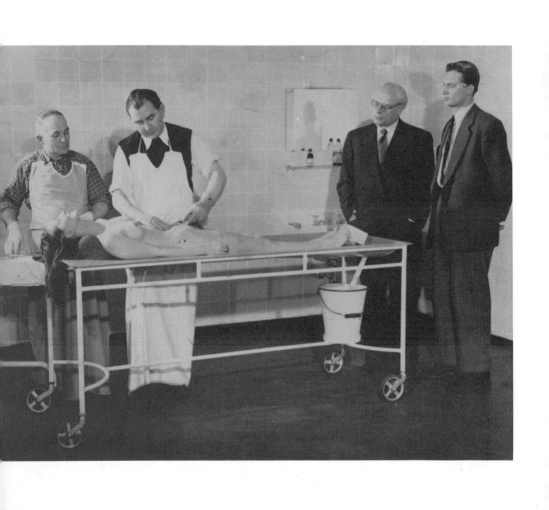

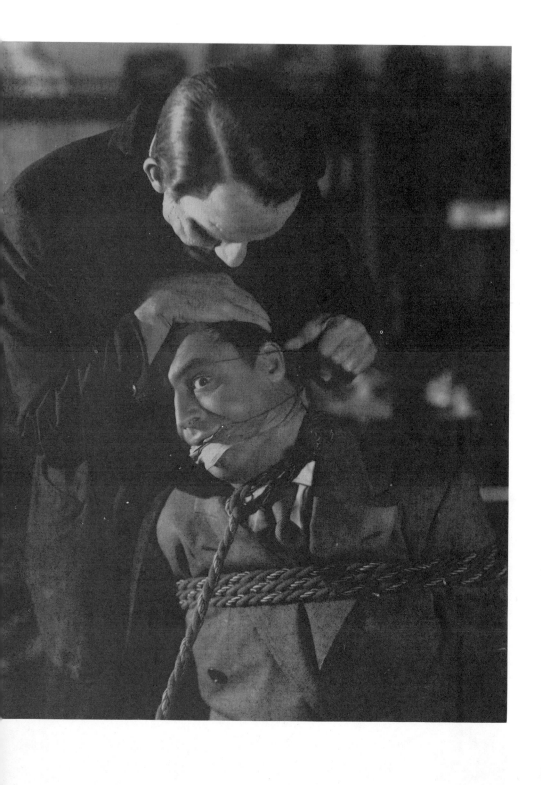

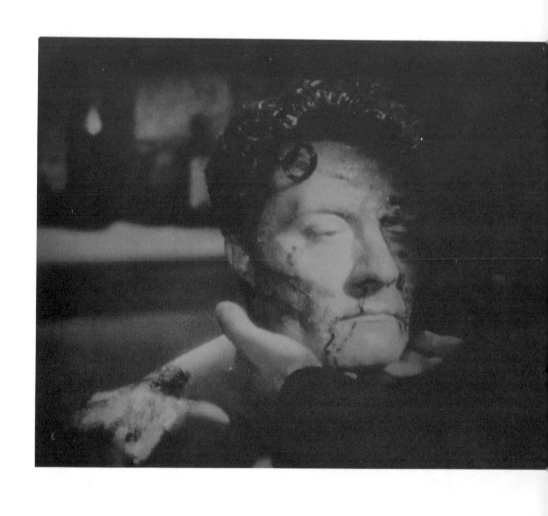

VAMPIRES

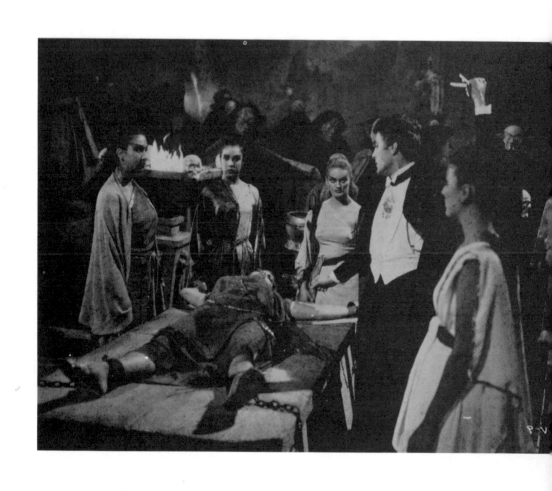

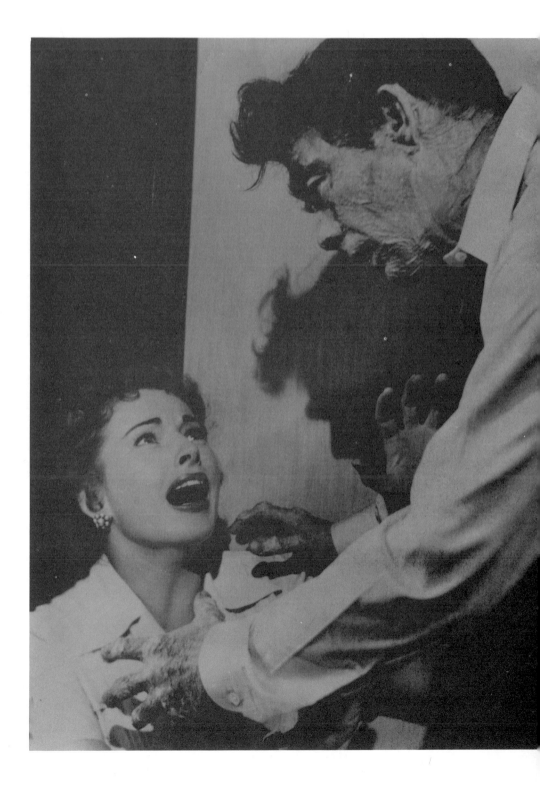

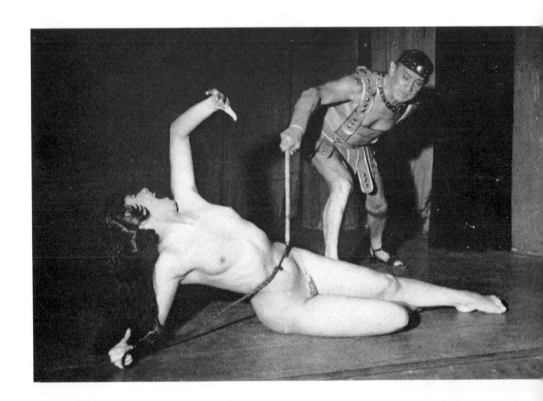

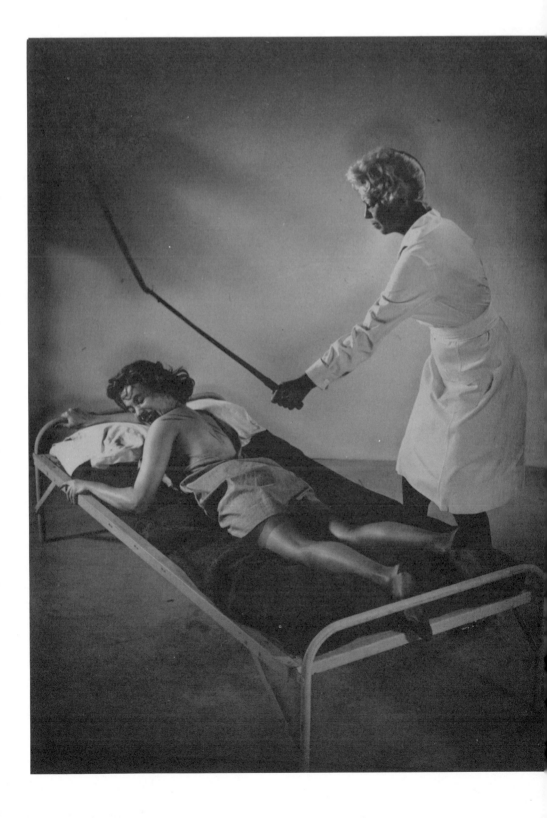

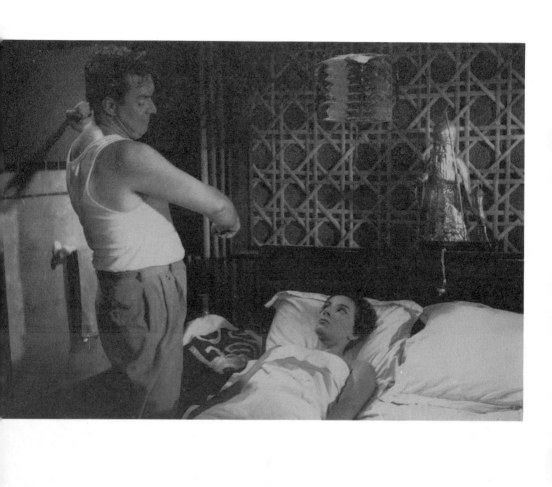

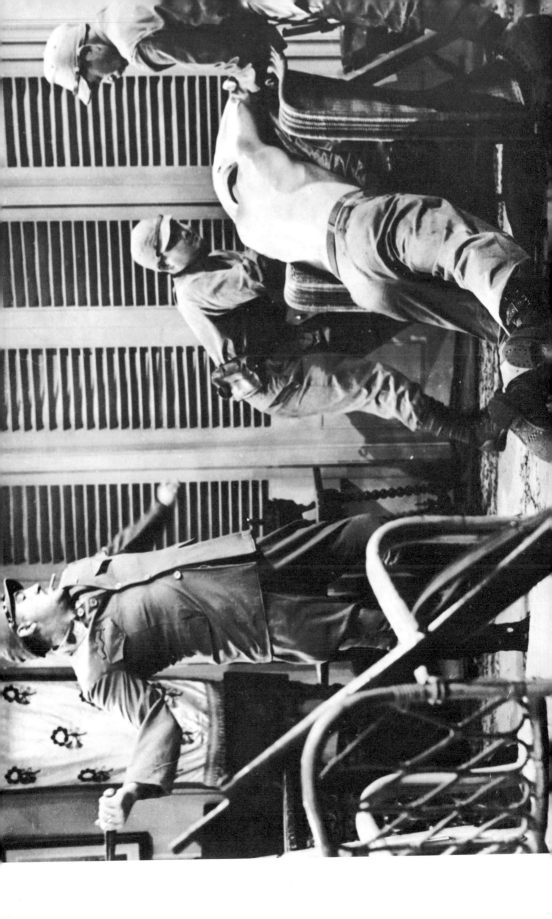

216-92

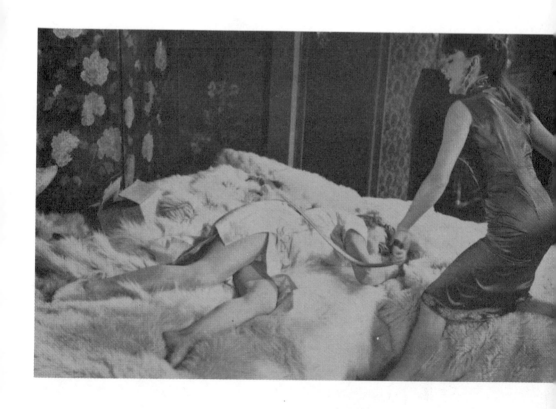